Compassion in the Court

Compassion in the Court

LIFE-CHANGING STORIES
FROM AMERICA'S NICEST JUDGE

FRANK CAPRIO

BenBella Books, Inc.

Dallas, TX

BenBella Books, Inc.
8080 N. Central Expressway
Suite 1700
Dallas, TX 75206
benbellabooks.com
Send feedback to feedback@benbellabooks.com

BenBella is a federally registered trademark.

Printed in the United States of America
10 9 8 7 6 5 4 3 2

Library of Congress Control Number: 2024030755
ISBN 9781637746035 (hardcover)
ISBN 9781637746042 (electronic)

Editing by Vy Tran
Copyediting by Elizabeth Degenhard
Proofreading by Lisa Story and Rebecca Maines
Text design and composition by Aaron Edmiston
Cover design by Sarah Avinger
Cover photo by Soozie Sundlun
Printed by Lake Book Manufacturing

To my parents, Filomena and Antonio "Tup" Caprio

Contents

PART TWO—COMPASSION

PART THREE—RESPECT

PART FOUR—UNDERSTANDING

In My Courtroom

Of all the jobs I've had in my life, including being a teacher, a lawyer, a councilman, a restaurateur, and a fight promoter, the one that I enjoyed the most was being a judge. Sitting on the bench was not work to me; rather, it was a privilege that never got old and that I truly loved.

Yet I was never quite comfortable with the title "Judge." It conjures an image of a person sitting above others, wearing a black robe, and banging a gavel, ordained somehow to pass judgment on the people standing before them. I never saw my role as an arbiter of innocence or guilt. I always tried to see individuals for who they were and make decisions based on all that I could learn about them and the events that brought them to my courtroom and what best allowed them to move forward when they left.

For thirty-eight years, I had the privilege of being a judge for the Providence Municipal Court. I typically heard cases involving traffic, parking, city ordinance, and other low-level citations. Into

1

my courtroom came thousands and thousands of people of all ages, from all walks of life, with all sorts of life experiences.

The men and women who appeared before me were often immigrants and first-generation Americans who didn't speak English well, if at all. They were often the working poor, trying to make a living on low wages. Many had young children; some were still students themselves. The defendants often arrived with their family and friends. Sometimes what was most noticeable was who was *not* there: an ex, a father, someone who was in jail at the time.

For most of these people, coming to stand before me in court was their first encounter with the judicial and American legal system. Many came from backgrounds where they had lost faith in government and were accustomed to institutions coming down hard on them without regard for their personal circumstances. Generally, most people do not look forward to interacting with a judge, or any government entity. And for good reason. It's not fun to wait in long lines at the motor vehicle registry, to be placed on hold for extended time on a phone call with city services, or to face a judge for a parking ticket received in front of the hospital while your child was in the emergency room.

If I had to rule just by the strict definition of the law, I probably would have dispensed harsher justice over the course of my thirty-eight years on the bench. However, my judicial and personal philosophy is simple: treat everyone with kindness, consideration, and dignity.

In my courtroom, we tried our hardest not to embarrass anyone. We treated everyone with respect and showed empathy and compassion for their circumstances. We did our best to understand not just what happened in a specific case but *why* the person made the choices that landed them in court. I often began that process by asking what was going on in their lives. The answers were sometimes funny and sometimes troubling and very often touched my heart.

In my courtroom came the good, the bad, and those who had to choose which way they wanted their life to go. Being honest and showing that they were working hard to support their family or to better themselves often led to my dismissing a person's charges or reducing their fine. Taking responsibility, admitting their mistakes, and, on some occasions, making hard decisions about the people in their lives served those who stood before me much better than making excuses, lying, or seeing themselves as victims of circumstance or bad luck.

In my courtroom, I showed everyone the respect they deserved, the understanding they craved, and the compassion they needed. I strived to administer justice in a manner intended to help others. Because in helping others we teach them to exercise similar behaviors in their own lives and, possibly, in the lives of others. In countless small ways, I hope this helps the world become a better place.

I often say, "I don't wear a badge under my robe, I wear a heart."

Although I am a judge, I am also a person of faith and I believe that in the end we will all be judged, and it will not be by how much we have taken, but by how much we have given. It will not be by the dreams we made come true for ourselves, but by those we made come true for others. Ultimately, we will be judged by the hope we inspire in the hopeless and the difference we made in the lives that we touched.

The people who came into my courtroom were real, as were the problems and challenges they faced. Although we began filming the

I'm not here on the court to be an entertainer.
My primary role is to do justice.

I never threw the book at anyone!

courtroom for informational and educational purposes, I was not playing to the camera or doing anything for show. I just did my job as judge and spoke from the heart, tempered by my life experience and that of my family.

While I am honored that millions and millions of people have watched our court proceedings on TV or on a multitude of platforms, services, and devices, what I really hope is that our viewers were inspired to be better people.

In the following pages, I will share accounts of the many remarkable individuals who came into my court. The cases themselves are not matters for law journals or the Supreme Court. These are not crimes of moral turpitude, just traffic and parking violations. Most often, the defendants and I spent minutes, not hours, together. And, with a few exceptions, I never saw them again. Yet the circumstances that brought them to court are real-world challenges from which we can all learn.

What I hope to demonstrate is that having compassion, respect, and understanding for ourselves and for others can yield more positive results in business and in life.

Empathy and compassion, often mentioned in this book, are similar in spirit but are not the same. Put simply: empathy is our ability to feel another's pain; compassion motivates us to help them.

Respect comes in many forms: it can be given, it can be received, and it often needs to be earned. There is also a difference between the respect you show others and having self-respect—both important, and all of which we will discuss.

Finally, understanding, as we will use it in this book, refers to when a person understands their situation and themselves such that they can make the right decisions for themselves as well as toward others.

Compassion, respect, and understanding are a powerful combination and a life-changing recipe for success and happiness. For some people, these traits come naturally; while for others, they can take time and effort to practice. For me, transforming these ideals into actions and aspirations into habits usually involves putting myself in the shoes of someone else and then relating it to my experiences with family members, relatives, friends, business associates, and the people who came into my courtroom—and trust me, I have a lot of experiences. After all, life-changing recipes for success and happiness don't come from nowhere.

So, before we get into the court cases, let me tell you about myself, my big immigrant family, and my personal history. You'll see how it all came together to inform the person I became and the values I hold dear, how those values affected the decisions I made in the cases that came before me, and how making decisions with compassion, respect, and understanding can have a multiplying and life-changing effect.

PART ONE

My Family Made Me the Person I Am Today

CHAPTER 1

From Teano to Providence

I recently went to Teano, a small town in southern Italy, and found my father's birth certificate. The document revealed that my grandfather, Antonio Caprio Sr., was illiterate. Here's a translation from the original Italian record:

> In the year 1908, the 25th of September, at 8 AM, in the office of the municipality in front of me, Lawyer Carmine Leonardo, Mayor and Civil Status Officer of the Municipality of Teano, appeared Antonio Caprio, aged 30, profession "daily" (a worker paid per day in agriculture), resident in Teano, who declared that at 7 PM on the day 24th of this month (September) in the house located in "Vico Primo e Michele," without a house number, from his wife, Carolina Pietropaolo, cohabitant, a male child was born that he showed me and to which he gave the name Antonio.

Witnesses present in the same moment are: Cosimo Zilella, 26-year-old worker in factory, Giuseppe Gliottone, 40-year-old baker, both residents in this town.

I have read this document to those present. I sign on behalf of the declarant and witnesses because they are all illiterate.

It turns out that Antonio and his two close friends who served as witnesses to my father's birth could not even read or write their own names. After completing the registration, they took my father, Antonio Jr., back to a one-room home with a dirt floor and just one window, where Antonio and Carolina Caprio had been living with their four older children. Though the Caprios eventually immigrated to the United States, their house in Teano stands to this day, still a small undistinguished building with a dirt floor. It is hard for me to imagine that seven people had all lived there.

In 1910, Antonio left Naples by himself, leaving his wife and small children in Teano, on a mission to start a better life for his family in the United States. Two years later, on May 31, 1912, Carolina, along with her eldest and youngest sons, Luigi and Antonio Jr., embarked on the ocean vessel *Venezia*, destined for Providence, Rhode Island. Eventually, the other three children would reunite with the family in Providence. My grandparents would have five more children in America. The twelve of them—two parents and ten children—all squeezed into a tenement apartment on Federal Hill, the Italian section of Providence.

I visited Teano, Italy, in 2022 and saw the home where my father, Tup, lived with his parents and four older brothers.

My grandmother, Maria Dello Iacono, with me
(*left*) and my brother, Antonio Jr. (*right*)

The development of Federal Hill dates to 1788 when businessman Amos Atwell, among others, began to transform the neighborhood into an urban center, building storefronts and homes. The same year, a group of Federalists took to the hill to celebrate the ratification of the Constitution by nine of the thirteen states.

The party became a brawl when anti-Federalists showed up in strength to stop the celebration, a testament to the reason that Rhode Island was the last state to ratify the Constitution despite being the first colony to have declared independence. When Rhode Island finally joined the union two years later in 1790, another celebration was held on what was by then called Federal Hill.

During the nineteenth century, most immigrants to Providence had been Irish, particularly after the Irish famine in 1845. By 1885, Irish Americans made up 56 percent of Providence's population. As further waves of Irish immigration arrived, worker housing, often cheap and poorly built, rose on Federal Hill.

However, beginning in the 1880s, there were increasing waves of Italian immigration. It is estimated that between 1885 and 1920, about five million Italians immigrated to the United States. Among them are some 55,000 Italians who came to Providence on the Fabre Line of ships that included the *Venezia*, on which my grandparents came to this country.

Why did so many Italians leave their homeland during this time? In the mid-nineteenth century, northern Italy was unified under King Victor Emmanuel II. On October 26, 1860, Victor Emmanuel famously met with Italian revolutionary Giuseppe Garibaldi, who had conquered Naples and Sicily, in Teano, in a bid to gain control of the southern states and form a united Italy. He succeeded and became the first king of Italy.

The *Venezia*'s manifest includes the names of my grandmother, Carolina Pietropaola, my uncle Luigi, and my father, Antonio Jr., who sailed from Naples, Italy, to Providence, Rhode Island, in May 1912.

Southern Italy, however, which was mainly agricultural, continued to suffer from a feudal system of landowners and corrupt and inept government. Jobs were few, pay was little, and there was no room for advancement. These factors drove many southern Italians to risk everything to come to the United States as part of the large first wave of Italian immigration.

Like other immigrants, not all would be allowed to enter. A sign of illness, physical or psychological, could be reason enough to turn a prospective immigrant back to their home country. Interestingly, there was a special rule when it came to Italian immigrants: immigration officials were instructed that if an immigrant showed irrational or hot-tempered behavior, they were to be denied entry to America, *unless* they were Italian—because such behavior was considered a natural cultural characteristic!

So many ships came from Italy that the arriving immigrants were often met at the docks by members of the Italian Catholic Church dioceses and immigrant welfare organizations, as well as by their relatives. Many Italian immigrants would go to meet the ships to see if anyone had arrived from their village and if they needed a place to stay. My grandmother was among those who regularly did this.

From the port of Providence, many immigrants would then find a home on Federal Hill, a section of Providence close to downtown but on the other side of the Providence River. Three- to four-story tenement walk-up apartments, meant to house one family per floor, were soon crowded with other family members and neighbors from Italy, sometimes with several families living together on one floor.

At the time, Irish immigrants had the upper hand on available jobs. They had been in Providence longer, and they spoke English. Even the street names in Providence, such as McEvoy, Jones, and Bradford, were all English and Irish. However, as the Irish got better jobs and moved to other neighborhoods, the Italian immigrants moved in, making Federal Hill Providence's Italian neighborhood.

Back then, when you would look for a job, there would be anti-Italian signs saying "Guineas not welcome" or "Wops not welcome." There was no war over it. There were no protests, no news stories, no organized resistance, no lawsuits. That was just the way it was.

Unable to find work, my grandfather, Antonio Sr., who spoke little English, sold fruit from a pushcart.

Often, after a hard day's work that began before dawn, he would gather with his friends, all Italian immigrants and mostly pushcart peddlers, in their very own social club to drink homemade wine. On one occasion, they turned rowdy.

My grandmother, Carolina, was at home when she received a visit from one of her neighbors saying, "Your husband is in jail. He got arrested."

My grandmother, who spoke even less English than my grandfather, was in a panic, imagining the worst. She was unfamiliar with the American judicial system and feared a long jail sentence for her husband. "My husband, he's going to be in jail for five years" is what she believed. Her neighbor had told her to be in court the next morning.

My father, Antonio Jr., was a young boy at the time. But he could speak English. My grandmother told him he had to go to court with her to be her interpreter.

"Papa's going to be in court; he got arrested," she explained. "He's in jail."

My grandmother assumed she would have to pay a huge fine to get my grandfather out because that was the way it worked in Italy. She had no idea how much it would cost, but she knew it was more than she had.

I cannot fathom the fear and helplessness that my grandmother felt at that very moment. She had ten children by then, and her husband would not be able to help support their family from a jail cell. Her life would be irretrievably destroyed if her husband was sent to jail. This was a catastrophe. This was a tragedy.

She went to all the fruit peddlers that they knew, explaining the situation and asking to borrow money, pleading in Italian, begging, that she needed the money to get her husband out of jail.

Though none of the fruit peddlers had money to spare, they all gave what they could to help my grandmother. She hoped it would be enough.

The next morning, Carolina put on three dresses because it was cold. She had the pack of cash from the fruit cart peddlers inside her innermost dress.

My grandmother and my father walked to the courthouse, which was not far away from where they lived on Federal Hill. She was extremely nervous and worried. She had never been in a courtroom or even a court building. She had no idea what to expect. It was as if she had traveled to another planet.

They were waiting in the courtroom when the court officers brought up my grandfather from his cell. He looked terrible: disheveled, unshaven, his clothes wrinkled, looking like he hadn't slept at all. The bailiffs sat him on a bench.

Everything about the courtroom was intimidating: the judge sitting on a raised platform, the bailiff with a gun, the American flag, the seal of the state of Rhode Island, the oak-paneled room, and all the protocols of the courtroom, which were totally foreign to my grandmother.

Carolina could only imagine this going from bad to worse. She whispered to my father in Italian, telling him he needed to speak up when they called my grandfather's case—to say we are here, and that we can pay to take him home. My father nodded in agreement.

The judge came into the courtroom. He was tall and ruddy-looking. My father recalled him as "a great white-haired Irishman." He looked like every Italian immigrant's nightmare.

At which point, my grandmother, unable to contain her anxiety a second longer, jumped up out of her seat, without letting my father speak, screaming in her broken English, "Judge-a! Judge-a! Please, please, judge-a! No-a da jail! Please, no-a da jail!" She reached into her dress and pulled out her pack of money, saying, "I gotta da money! I pay-a! Please-a, no-a da jail!"

At this point, my father was afraid the judge might have my grandmother arrested, too.

The judge, noticing my father there, asked if he spoke English and if he could translate for him. My father said he could.

The judge said, "Tell your mother her husband is a good man who works hard to support his family and he had a bad night. I understand that she needs him at home. So, I'm going to send him to be with his children, and I want her to cook him a good meal."

Before my father finished relaying the message in Italian, my grandmother was already saying to the judge, "Thank-a you, Judge-a! Thank-a you, Judge-a!" She was even blowing him kisses as she left the courtroom.

The way that judge treated my grandmother and my grandfather, with tremendous compassion and respect, without any prejudice or bias because they were immigrants or because they were poor or because he was Irish and they were Italian, and with a great understanding of human foibles, made a tremendous impression on my grandparents and on my father.

That one encounter gave my father tremendous respect for the law and the American judicial system, and my father passed along that respect to me. My father would tell me this story often as I was growing up. That "great white-haired Irishman" judge was practically a saint in our household, since what could have been the worst experience for my grandfather, grandmother, and father had a happy ending. The judge's behavior was the ideal, and in many ways, that case is responsible for why my father thought I should become a lawyer.

In 1985, almost seventy years later, in a wonderful twist of fate, I was sworn in as a judge in that very same court, the Providence Municipal Court, and would dispense justice to the new waves of immigrants for almost forty years. Why I became a judge and how I would dispense justice in my courtroom was influenced by my grandparents' and my father's experience in court.

When I was on the bench and I looked at a defendant, particularly an immigrant who stood before me with fear and uncertainty in their eyes, what I saw was my grandfather and my grandmother.

I hoped to treat each person with the same compassion, respect, and understanding that the judge gave my grandparents.

Unfortunately, my grandfather died when he was only fifty-two, leaving my grandmother with ten children to raise. She was a force of nature. She took over my grandfather's pushcart, and she also sold grapes for people to make wine during the season, and all the kids helped. None of her children could play with their friends or participate in organized activities after school; they had to help their mother.

Carolina Caprio bathes her grandson in front of what is now the Caprio Building in Providence, Rhode Island.

My grandmother and her generation of immigrants didn't want their children and other Italians to forget their cultural traditions and heritage, so communal organizations, often women's groups, gathered people from the same region, sometimes the same town, to protect their values while at the same time providing social and health services that integrated them into the American social fabric.

On Federal Hill, community organizations took over what was initially called the Sprague House, which later became known as Federal Hill House. Over time, Federal Hill House provided recreation facilities, including volleyball and basketball, doctors' services, a medical clinic for the poor, and even a women's lactation station. Federal Hill House is still in operation, although no longer at its original location.

Nonetheless, the most important community center was the church. There were two Italian parishes on Federal Hill, Holy Ghost and Our Lady of Mount Carmel, which was where my family attended, and where the priests spoke Italian as well as English and performed mass in Latin.

When my Uncle Pippy (Giuseppe) was a baby, he became sick. My grandmother prayed to the patron saints of her village, Saint Anthony and Saint Paris (also known as Saint Paride), that her child would survive. When he did, she decided she would honor the saints.

She formed her own women's communal organization, the Society of Women from Teano (*La Societa Femina di Teano*). They would march in church processions on June 13, the feast day for Saint Anthony, and on August 5, the feast day for Saint Paride. They marched in Franciscan habits, carrying the society's custom-designed flag.

Many of the women in *La Societa* did not speak or read English. Most of them did not know how to become American citizens. My grandmother, who spoke little English herself, directed the women to Federal Hill House, where the citizenship process was explained to them in Italian.

Once they became citizens, my grandmother would encourage them to vote. Over time, *La Societa* became a large organization with my grandmother being able to reliably deliver large numbers of votes from Federal Hill, which made her a political force in Providence and Rhode Island. She understood that a woman's influence at home could extend to politics. So, each woman in *La Societa* was

Carolina Caprio (*center*, marked with a 1) leads
her Society of Women from Teano.

generally able to deliver the votes for their entire family for the chosen candidate.

My grandmother became a particular favorite of J. Howard
McGrath, Rhode Island's governor, who went on to become U.S.
Solicitor General, a U.S. senator, and Attorney General of the
United States. On several occasions she went to his house for din-
ner, and when my grandmother fell sick, he came to visit. You can
imagine the scene when the official car of the Attorney General of
the United States, with the flags, pulled up to our house on Federal
Hill. No one had ever seen anything like that in our neighborhood.
But it was a sign of the affection and respect people had for her.

I always admired Senator McGrath for his loyalty to my grandmother, and I also learned a valuable political lesson by watching

him. He practiced what Thomas "Tip" O'Neill became known for decades later: all politics is local. Even after he had become Attorney General of the United States and his talents and attention were focused on national issues and leading the U.S. Department of Justice, he remained a friend to my grandmother. He respected her as a pillar of her community, even though she was an immigrant who didn't speak English or have any financial resources and struggled as a single mother of ten children.

Some people have said about me that I "never forgot where I came from" by the way I relate to the plight of the people that appear in my court. The truth is, I learned the importance of staying grounded from people like J. Howard McGrath and my grandmother.

⚖

Because I had a front-row seat to my grandparents' and parents' experiences, I have great empathy for immigrants. I have always found that immigrants, each with their own cultural heritage, make our country richer in every way.

As proud as I am of my heritage, I am also very proud of Providence and Rhode Island's reputation as a place of refuge. Roger Williams founded the colony of Rhode Island as an area that was open to the outside world. In fact, early maps of Rhode Island have the word "refugio" or "refuge" on them. Rhode Island remains a place that is enriched by its diversity. It doesn't matter if your name is O'Reilly, Johnson, Rodriguez, Caprio, Klein, Quan, or Mohammed—our state, our city, and our courtroom welcome you.

During my almost forty years on the bench, a lot of immigrants came before me. Young, old, single, married, with children or not. They were from Europe, Latin or Central America, and from countries in the Middle East, such as Syria and Iraq. Many came from countries where life was exceedingly difficult. They were hardworking people and often devoted parents who wanted a better life for their children. And to a person, they were grateful to be in America. I must pause here and say this again because it is so important: to a person, they were grateful to be in America. So often, those of us born in the United States take for granted how fortunate we are.

I identify with them because of my own immigrant heritage, and how lucky I am that my grandparents and parents decided to come to this country from Italy more than a hundred years ago.

I must tell one last funny story about this portion of my family history. Many years ago, I got a call from the president of one of the Providence banks who was on a committee to refurbish the Statue of Liberty. He asked me to join the committee and help raise funds, which I did. To thank me, they offered to give me a private tour of the statue.

I arrived in New York with my good friend Mark Weiner, and we were taken by boat to Liberty Island, where the statue was inspiring and wonderful. On our way back, my host asked if we wanted to stop at Ellis Island. We did, and I found the experience so moving that when I returned to Providence, I immediately called my dad. I told him I wanted to have lunch to tell him all about it.

When we were seated at the restaurant, I was so excited. I said, "Dad, let me tell you the story of what I saw at Ellis Island." I told him that when we entered the arrivals hall, the old interview booths were still there. I touched the counter, and I touched the glass there. On the massive staircase that all the immigrants had to climb, I slowly went up the first five stairs and held on to the railing. I placed both hands on the railing. I touched each stair with my hands on the way down. It was a very emotional moment for me. And I said, "Dad, do you know why I did that?"

"No," he said, "I have no idea."

I told him I did so because I felt like I was transported in time. "I could see you there," I said. "I could actually feel your and grandma's feet on the steps and your fingers on the rail. I could feel the grooves of your fingerprints on the rail and channeled the fear and excitement of what it must have felt like for you to walk through that building." I had a difficult time not bursting into tears in the middle of the restaurant. "That's why I did that."

My father heard my voice quivering and was blankly staring at me. He was completely nonplussed.

"Frank," he said, as he shook his head and put his spoon back in his bowl of soup. "We landed in Providence."

Wait. What? I had not realized that there was a port of entry for immigrants in Providence. But, indeed, there was! My whole life, the narrative in my head had been of my family arriving at Ellis Island! Once again, my father was teaching me to do my homework.

I learned that there was a port of entry not only in Providence but also in other locations on the East Coast such as Boston and Philadelphia. Ellis Island was just one port of arrival.

Today, when I tell people that my family left Italy and settled in Providence, I usually mention that the ship they were on actually *arrived* in Providence. As far as my family's American heritage goes, the Caprios are really from Providence, straight off the dock!

CHAPTER 2

My Father Tup

y father, Antonio Caprio Jr., was the major influence on
my life and that of my children. As a child, he only got as
far as the seventh grade before he had to work full-time
with my grandfather on the pushcart to help support the family.

Everyone called my father Tup or "Tup of Toffee." The story was
that one day while my father was working with my grandfather on
the pushcart, they had gone to the wholesale farm market at 5 AM
on a frigid winter morning to get the day's fruit. They took their
pushcarts to the street where they were allowed to set up their stall,
but they had to wait until 7 AM when the policeman blew his whistle before they could all rush to grab a prized spot.

On that morning, it was very cold outside, so my grandfather
waited in a coffee shop until my father had secured a place for the
pushcart. My father braved the sub-zero temperatures and biting
wind to try to get a jump on a good spot for the pushcart as soon as
the whistle blew. He waited and waited like a sprinter at the starting

Tup on the pushcart, circa 1928

block anticipating the starting pistol. Finally, the whistle blew, he lifted the handles of the pushcart, which was heavy with the day's products, raced to the designated area, and secured his spot. Once there, he set up the fruit into a neat pyramid.

Afterward, my father arrived at the coffee shop to tell my grandfather the cart was all set. My grandfather was there with all his friends and the guy behind the counter said, "What can I get you?"

What my father wanted was a cup of coffee, but his face was so frozen from the bitterly cold morning that when he opened his mouth what came out was, "A tup. A tup of toffee."

From that day on, for the rest of his life, he was known as Tup.

When someone introduced him to another person, they would say, "I'd like you to meet my friend, Tup Caprio." My mother called him Tup. His brothers, sisters, friends, coworkers, and the whole neighborhood called him Tup. His fifty nephews and nieces, and their spouses and children, called him Uncle Tup. My two brothers and I were the only people that were privileged enough to call him a different name, and that was "Dad."

If someone came to Federal Hill and asked a local if Antonio Caprio was around, the person would not know who they were talking about. However, if they asked for Tup, *everyone* knew exactly who they meant. This was true until the day he died.

When the Depression came, no one had money to buy fruit or to maintain the fruit stand. Tup left the fruit-peddling business. He was fortunate, however, because he got a job from the Works Progress Administration (WPA), the program President Franklin D. Roosevelt enacted to put Americans to work.

The WPA put him to work as a laborer at the Quonset Point Naval Station, the shipyard in North Kingston, Rhode Island, most famous for developing the Quonset hut. In 1941, it became an air station for World War II naval pilots.

After his stint at the naval station, Tup found employment with Hood, a dairy company, as a milk deliveryman. That was considered incredibly good employment for an Italian in those days. Tup was perfect for the job because it involved going to people's apartments and houses on Federal Hill, delivering their milk, picking up their empties, and collecting their milk bills. Many of his customers had also come from Teano.

Tup wearing Hood's milk delivery uniform

It was not easy work. He had about one hundred families on his route, all of them living in three-story tenement apartment houses with no elevators. He would have to carry the crates of milk in thick glass bottles up those stairs several times a week to deliver the milk and pick up the empties to bring back to the company, to be cleaned and refilled. He was so strong that he could grab a crate of twelve bottles with one hand and then move it wherever it needed to go in the truck. All day he was moving the crates for the next delivery.

Aside from great physical stamina, it took a good deal of logistical planning to do the job efficiently and well. Tup would often say that if you could successfully run a milk truck, you could operate a multinational company. Tup was responsible for delivering several grades of milk, including regular, pasteurized, homogenized, select, grade A, and Guernsey (the most expensive); he also delivered eggs, eggnog, orange juice, and other products that were perishable. The deliveries had to be timely, often before dawn.

The deliveries also had to be organized by the specific order of each customer, his route, and by the location of the apartment within the house. Tup catered to a hundred customers at a time, with a hundred different orders. He also had to track the billing and the payments, receive money, and make change, well before the days of credit cards, Zelle, PayPal, and Venmo. Payments were all in cash, and he took in a lot of coins.

Once the truck was on the road, it was too late to make changes. The most important work was done at the company's Providence offices, where the orders were reviewed, and the milk crates organized and strategically placed in the truck. There were no bar codes, computers, internet, or logistics programs to assist. It was all on Tup to balance all those responsibilities every morning.

Tup did his work flawlessly by using his innate talents, which were his work ethic, honesty, intelligence, and common sense. These are the qualities that enabled him to excel at his job, none of which can be taught in a classroom. My two brothers and I had a front-row seat to learn as much as we could from our father's daily grind. Those lessons would serve me well throughout every aspect of my life.

If it was summer, Tup might bring the milk into the house of his customers and place it in their refrigerator. If it was winter and it was cold enough, he would leave the milk bottles in the hallway in front of the apartment. But often enough, the customers knew Tup and would invite him inside for a cup of coffee, and he would sit with them. Sometimes they might say, "You want something to eat with that?" And Tup would have a bite with them.

Many of his customers were our neighbors on Federal Hill, and many of my classmates and friends also lived in the area. Most households had children in them. Occasionally, some customers were unable to pay at the end of the week for the milk that was delivered. Hood's policy was that delivery was to cease immediately if the customer fell behind for a certain period of time, until they caught up. Tup viewed that as an extreme measure for any family that was struggling to make ends meet. After all, throughout his life, his parents routinely had to figure out how to get by for periods of time with no money at all. It was part of life as a poor, hardworking immigrant pursuing the American Dream.

Also, milk, eggs, and the other products that Hood delivered were not readily available in the butcher shop, produce store, or small markets on Federal Hill. Supermarkets were not yet prevalent. Most shopping was done by walking from store to store in your neighborhood. So, stopping delivery was a drastic event.

Tup had his own policy when it came to "stopping the milk," particularly if there were children in the home. He would take some of his own money, which he really didn't have to spare, and pay it toward the customer's bill. He would tell the management that the customer was doing their best to make partial payments. So, the delivery would continue. Hood eventually caught on to Tup's "customer relations policy" and, to their credit, saw its wisdom and adopted it throughout the company.

Tup's logic served me every day I was on the bench. Many of the people who appeared before me in court had cars that had a "boot" that the city had placed on one of the tires for nonpayment of parking violations. The law required that I not remove the boot until the parking fines were paid. But if I did that, often the person could never afford to retrieve their car; or, if they paid the tickets in full, that meant they had no money for groceries for their children. I just couldn't do that for the same reasons Tup couldn't stop delivering the milk. So, I would routinely allow people to institute a payment plan, even if it was only $5 per week. I would also use donations from a special fund (more about that later) to pay the fines.

Thousands of people who came before me were the unwitting beneficiary of my father's wisdom and generosity, which I learned by watching him operate his own "multinational company" milk truck.

Tup's determination to help good people avoid hardship had a profound and lasting effect on me. Never punish someone, particularly a child, because they are poor.

CHAPTER 3

The Privilege of Being Poor

I was born on November 24, 1936, at the height of the Depression. When my mother, Filomena, married my father, Tup, they had zero money—I mean *zero*. As my brother once said, "They didn't even have lint in their pockets!"

Yet happiness is not measured by how much money you have in the bank or the size of your house. I know this is true because I had a very happy childhood despite being poor. To me, my childhood was a gift.

I had the good fortune of being born into a large and loving Italian American family. We didn't have money, but I had the privilege of eating home-cooked meals every night with my family around the table, sharing our day's activities. I had the privilege of learning that a hug from my mother was more valuable than anything that could be purchased at a store. And I had the privilege of having the most loving parents, and that, simply put, is priceless. All that they had they gave me, and they put their hearts and souls into shaping me as a human being; and whatever I have accomplished to this day is because of my privileged life.

Our apartment was on the second floor of a clapboard house. It was in the rear of the building and had a view of the great white granite dome of the Rhode Island State House, which looks like a smaller version of the U.S. Capitol in Washington, D.C. Our apartment was a cold-water flat, which means that we did not have hot running water. For a hot shower, I had to go once a week to the local bath hall a few blocks away or to school in the locker room, not at my own house. To wash dishes and clothes, my mother would have to boil water and fill up the sink.

When I was in high school, we finally put a hot water tank in our apartment. Life got a little easier, yet it was amazing that we never felt deprived in all those years that we didn't have hot water. It was just a part of life. We felt fortunate that the bath house and school gym were not too far away, as many of our friends had a longer walk.

We used oil stoves. The oil was stored in the building's basement, which had a dirt floor. To refill the stove, we had to carry the oil drum, or a bucket filled with oil, up and down wooden stairs. Over the years those stairs became soaked with kerosene, as a little would spill on each trip up the stairs, making every home a fire hazard. It's incredible that in an era where most people smoked cigarettes and men smoked cigars, there were not many house fires caused by a lit cigarette dropped down the back stairwell.

Being poor may have prevented us from having material items, but it did not impact my parents' ability to teach us the most valuable life lessons. Certainly, having more money or living in a better home does not guarantee better or more supportive parents. I know that from what I saw as a kid.

One time when I was eight or nine years old, I was helping my father on the milk truck when my father had me bring the milk up to a family. I didn't know them, but their son was in my class at school. It was terribly cold outside, I was freezing, and I had been awake since 4 AM. I was hoping to warm up for a few minutes in their apartment and hoping they might even offer me something hot to drink or eat, as would often happen on the milk route.

As I approached the door, I could smell the soothing aroma of toast in the morning. I could feel the immediate rush of heat as soon as their apartment door opened. I saw my classmate sitting at the kitchen table having his breakfast, and I was sure he would recognize me and invite me to join him. But then I quickly realized that wasn't going to happen: his father was screaming at him, and he was crying.

The father saw me standing there with the milk crate in my hands and my eyes wide open with anticipation of being invited in. I had a fleeting thought that my presence would stop whatever argument was happening in their home, and that the father would smile at me and offer me something warm.

The father paused and looked at me. Then he pointed his finger inches away from my face and turned his head back toward his son, who was still crying, and said, "Stop crying! You don't know how good you've got it. You could be like that kid there who has to carry milk bottles in the freezing cold."

I didn't know what to do. My young mind was racing. Should I stick up for myself and talk back to the father? Should I console my classmate? Should I allow myself to start crying, as I felt like doing? Should I go get my father to teach this mean man a lesson?

I did not say anything. I just left the bottles there and continued on with my duties. But it hurt me to have someone talk about me that way when I was standing right there. What had I done to deserve that? Bring his milk to his home for him? His behavior was so unlike the other families on our route. I will never forget that.

However, when I had a chance to think, I realized how lucky I was compared to that boy. Sure, he lived in a nice place, with plenty of heat, but he had a mean father. He had a father who screamed at him and who made him cry.

In contrast, I had a kind father I got to spend time with, even when he was at work. I was surrounded by a loving, supportive family. It was tough to climb out of bed at 4 AM, in the freezing cold. But I looked forward to it because I knew that once I was up, I would get to hang out with my father and brother. Every day was an adventure on the streets of Federal Hill where, at that hour, we would basically have the world to ourselves.

I wouldn't have traded places with that boy for all the money in the world.

In a white, button-up shirt standing in front of my father, Tup, in the suspenders, with my older brother, Antonio, in a suit and tie, and my mother, next to him, at a birthday party, circa 1944

CHAPTER 4

My Brother, My Hero, Anthony

My mother worked hard to keep our apartment clean and to create a warm and inviting atmosphere at our house so that when you walked through the door at the end of a long day, you felt at home. Still, despite her efforts, we faced challenges. There were always situations that were just beyond our control. For example, in winter, our house was never warm enough, particularly at night. It was common to wear clothes to bed. Anthony, my older brother by two years, and I shared a bed, and that also helped us stay warm.

During the day, Anthony and I worked on the milk truck with my dad. When it got very cold, the company Dad worked for gave him a big, thick, quilted blanket to put on the milk so it would not freeze, but sometimes it did anyway. Back then we delivered milk that wasn't homogenized, and the cream would rise to the top.

When it froze it would sometimes pop out of the container and some would get on the blanket.

At night, we would take that blanket home, and it went on the bed I shared with my brother, placed on top of the blanket we already had to keep us warm.

One night, we were asleep when suddenly I felt something on my leg. I woke up and, in the dim light that came through the window from the streetlights a block away, I saw that there was a giant rat staring right at me.

It was a scene from a horror movie. I quickly realized that the rat really wasn't interested in me or my brother. Rather, the rat was eating the milk that got on the blanket.

I was afraid of rats, so this scene terrified me to my core. I jumped up, screaming, "Anthony, Anthony, there's a rat in the bed!"

It was crazy. We were running around the room. The rat was a big bull, scurrying away toward the wall. But then Anthony did the unthinkable. As I was cowering in the corner of the room, Anthony's instinctive reaction was to protect me, his little brother, and he ran toward the rat! I couldn't believe what I was seeing. Anthony caught him before he got to the wall and killed the rat.

To this day, Anthony is my hero for doing that.

Life has a funny way of coming full circle. About forty years after Anthony killed the rat in our room, my youngest son, Paul, then a teenager, became interested in critters and reptiles. At various times he had iguanas, a lizard, and a tarantula spider.

One day, I was in my closet and saw something at eye level moving the clothes around. I turned on the light and, to my horror, I saw a thick, long boa constrictor wrapped up in the hangers. I didn't know that Paul had recently set up the bathtub in his bathroom as a snake enclosure. The snake had somehow moved the screen that was on top and escaped.

But that was not the worst part. When I went into Paul's bedroom, I saw that he also had a fish tank. Except it wasn't for fish. In it, he was keeping and breeding mice to feed to the snake.

The irony was priceless. I would have done anything to keep rodents out of our home when I was a kid, and here was my son, breeding mice inside the house!

CHAPTER 5

The Road Is Long

When I was about to graduate sixth grade, I came home one day with an autograph book. You didn't get a yearbook in sixth grade, but we would all bring autograph books to have them signed by our teachers and classmates.

As soon as I got home, I ran to my father with my autograph book and asked him to sign his name. In retrospect, I am sure my father was exhausted and wanted nothing more than to sit down and put his feet up. Even at the time, I was surprised that he didn't just open it to a blank page and sign his name, as everyone else had done at school.

What he did next was one of the most significant and impactful moments of my life. He took the book and looked down at me patiently for several moments. I was fixated on his gaze. I could see that he was deep in thought and had suddenly gotten very serious. Then, very deliberately and with great sincerity of spirit, he did more than sign the book. He wrote me a note in his less-than-perfect handwriting that said:

> *The street is wide. The road is long and very bumpy and very tough going. But I know you will proceed along it honorably with your head held high to the end of the highest learning.*
>   *From your dad, Antonio Caprio Jr.*

My father was not educated, but he had the soul of a poet. I have read that message a thousand times. His words touch me to this day, and I still find myself trying to make him proud and live up to his high expectations for me.

My father didn't attend school past the eighth grade, so, in his mind, my opportunities were already surpassing his. And he wanted me to know it, to provide hope and inspiration to his sixth-grade son. He treated this message like it was an official government document. His signature indicates the formality of his mindset. He didn't just sign it as "Dad." He wanted me, and anybody that would come to read his message, to know that it was written by Antonio Caprio Jr., as a father to his son. His prophetic message still motivates me to be honorable and hold my head high.

Strangely, even though I now have a college degree, a law degree, two honorary doctorate degrees, and almost ninety years of life experience, I have come to realize that the highest learning I ever received was at the foot of Antonio Caprio Jr.

To successfully navigate the wide street, and long and bumpy road, we all need a moral compass. I wasn't told how to be moral. I learned by watching others, most importantly the fine examples set by my mother and father. And, equally as influential was learning from some of the people around me who did not have a strong moral compass.

Once when my brother Anthony was only twelve years old, my mother gave him three dollars. To my father, three dollars was a lot of money. He asked my mother what it was for. She let him know she had given it to Anthony because he wanted the money for the rides at the local carnival. But afterward, my father found out my brother did not use the money to go on rides—he had gambled it away instead.

My father asked, "Where'd you gamble it?"

"The carnival," my brother said.

"Come on," my father told him. "Show me where you did this."

My father made me come along, too. We walked to the carnival, and Dad went up to the barker, the guy behind the counter, and said, "You." Again, "You, did you let this kid gamble? Did you take three dollars from him?"

The barker admitted he did. My father was a calm man, and he wasn't afraid of anyone. So, he simply said to the barker, "Oh. Give me back the three dollars." And he put out his hand and motioned for the barker to pay him.

The barker looked at my father and was about to say something when he stopped himself. Instead, he just gave my father back the three dollars.

My father took Anthony's hand, and we headed home. He told him, "Don't you ever do that again." Anthony never gambled again. That was how we were brought up.

CHAPTER 6

A Hand on Your Shoulder

There is one memory I have that helped define the trajectory of my life. From that moment on, I knew exactly what I was going to do, and that nothing was going to stop me. As with most significant events in my early life, my father was at the center of it.

It was a Monday, and it was freezing cold. We were at home about to have dinner, but to stay warm we kept the stove door open and had three chairs around it. We often did that. It's what poor people did. And being poor, with a house that didn't have sufficient heat, in a strange way made us closer as a family. We had to sit together around the stove to stay warm. Sometimes the radio would be on in the background. But most of the time, we would talk.

This Monday, my father stood next to me. He put his hand on my shoulder and said to me, "Someday you're going to be a lawyer.

You're a good talker. You're going to be a lawyer someday. But," he added, "there's one thing: you can't charge poor people like us. There will be enough rich people to pay you."

The words were direct, simple, and powerful. But when he placed his hand on my shoulder, I had a feeling that is hard to describe. Without his hand there, his words would not have had the same impact. It just felt like there was someone watching out for me, that I could feel confident that what he told me would come to pass.

Every day since, I still feel his hand on my shoulder. To this day, that moment meant so much to me. Its impact on me showed me that the more lives we can touch, the more hands we can place on shoulders to support others, the better the world would be. It is something I strived to do in my courtroom and in my life.

When a person appeared in my court who was trying to put their life back together after a history of bad decisions, drug addiction, or other difficulties, I would always encourage them to keep at their efforts, often reducing their fines or dismissing them. What I often said to them was, "I'm rooting for you." I could aways see in their eyes that those simple words had a great impact—letting them know they were not taking this journey alone and that others were there to support them, encourage them, even give them a break. That changed everything.

Sometimes that's all it takes to help someone who feels alone and vulnerable. Let them know that there is someone who cares about them and is putting a little wind in their sails. What good was levying fines they had incurred while struggling with addiction if that financial stress would be an impediment to their recovery and erase whatever motivation and momentum they may have had in trying to be productive again? Sometimes, a hand on the shoulder can make all the difference, as it did with me.

As adults, we should all take more time to lend a guiding hand. A gentle nudge can change a life for the better. And it is not hard to do. Letting someone know you care about their well-being and that you want them to be a good person can help them have a better life.

CHAPTER 7

The Importance of Showing Up

My father taught me that your character and your word is everything. Even as I was focused on myself, on graduating high school and going to college, Tup was always there to remind me of what was truly important.

When I was sixteen, I worked so many jobs that one might honestly lose track. Aside from helping my dad with the milk truck, I also worked shining shoes on the corner and delivering newspapers. I worked at a bowling alley setting the pins. I buffed cars in the body shop at the car dealership.

One time I was working at a restaurant on a Saturday night. I did not get out of the restaurant until 11 PM. When I got home my father said, "Anthony is leaving for Germany."

My older brother had been drafted and was stationed at Fort Dix, New Jersey. But he had gotten his deployment orders, and they were sending him to Germany.

"They're leaving at seven in the morning, so we have to make sure we go and see him," Dad said. I agreed to go with him. "We're going to leave the night before and get up very early to see him off. We'll stay in a hotel near the base."

The day before Anthony left, we drove down to New Jersey in my father's 1941 Chevrolet. It was a six-and-a-half-hour drive on difficult roads. For me, it was an adventure, an epic road trip that I got to share with my father. My mother had made us some sandwiches; when we got hungry, we ate those in the car or by the side of the road.

We found a nearby motel that charged $7 for a room about as big as a closet. This was a fortune for us to spend on something unplanned, so we both stayed in that tiny room.

I was so excited to see Anthony, I couldn't fall asleep. In my mind, I was picturing going to see him on the base, where he would be with his regiment in uniform; perhaps there would be a band and a parade, and we would be in the reviewing stand. I hoped to see his bunk and get to spend a few moments with him before he went off. That was how it was always portrayed in the movies, so I had no way to know anything different.

My father woke me up at 4:30 AM at the motel, saying, "We have to be there on time."

I drove us to the gate. My father pointed to the side of the road and said, "Okay, park over here."

I didn't understand why we were not going onto the base. Where was the reviewing stand, the band, and the soldiers at attention? I thought we must be in the wrong place, but I didn't want to say anything. So, we just stood there, by the side of the road just outside the gate in the darkness. As the hours wore on, I was hungry, thirsty, and tired. I also knew we had a long, tough drive back to Providence.

At 7 AM sharp, a bus came out of the gates at Fort Dix. My father exclaimed, "Here he is! Here he is!"

We could see my brother on the bus as it was driving by. He saw us and waved to us out of the window. He was excited and so were we. We enthusiastically waved back. And then he was gone.

That was it?

My father turned to me and said, "Ah, we saw him." We had no chance to spend time with him, to talk to him and give him a hug. But my father was as happy as could be.

"He knows we came and that is what matters," Dad said.

We got back in the car to make the more than six-hour drive back to Providence. We didn't say much on that trip back. We didn't need to. It became clear to me that this trip wasn't about us, or about me. It was about Anthony knowing we were there for him.

My brother told this story many times throughout his life. I got to see how important it was to him that we showed up. Tup set the bar high that day and taught me a lesson that Anthony and I never forgot.

Someone once said that "ninety percent of life is just showing up." I would amend that to "a good life is about showing up for others."

CHAPTER 8

Wrestling with a Decision

When I first went to high school, I was a short, skinny kid who weighed 112 pounds. Although I was small, I was determined, disciplined, and, most of all, tough, so my older brother, Anthony, a gifted athlete who excelled at playing football, told me that I should play football, too. I decided to play on the junior varsity team, and I'll be honest—I got killed. Everybody was bigger and stronger than me. I made the team, but I did not play that much because I was so small.

One day, the wrestling coach, Mr. Beachen, stopped me in the hall. He introduced himself and said I should come out for wrestling. I told Mr. Beachen that I didn't know anything about wrestling. To me, wrestling was something I saw on TV where guys in costumes, with names like Gorgeous George, were jumping on each other in a boxing ring.

Mr. Beachen said, "I hear that on the football field you're a pretty tough guy for your size."

"I don't know about that," I said. "I get beat up pretty bad."

"That's exactly why I'm talking to you," he said. "Now you're against these big guys. In wrestling, you only wrestle guys your own size." He convinced me to give wrestling a try.

The truth was that I was in good shape. Helping my father deliver milk crates and running up and down several flights of stairs in the tenements his customers lived in, carrying the full bottles up and the empties back down, turned out to be a good exercise program.

My senior year, I made the 138-pound wrestling weight class. Mr. Beachen, who had been the senior coach of wrestling and the dean of all wrestling coaches, retired and the school's athletic department had to hire a new coach. They asked the chemistry teacher, Carl Lauro, who had a couple of kids of his own and needed the extra money, to step in.

With that, Mr. Lauro became our coach. He guided us. He inspired us. He made sure we were organized and set our schedule for our workouts and matches. He used his organizational skills as a teacher and applied them to coaching. There was one major disconnect, however: he was not a wrestler himself, had never coached wrestling, and knew less than we did about the technical aspects of wrestling.

I suppose we could have complained, or we could have enjoyed the freedom to relax our training in favor of more horseplay. Instead, we took on the technical aspects ourselves. By now, as a senior, I knew the workout routine. We ran the practices like Marine sergeants and worked hard. We all knew the abilities of everyone on the team and when to push ourselves to train harder. We also spent time studying our opponents and strategizing on how best to win our matches. Mr. Lauro was there to motivate us and provide some adult supervision.

It was a hell of a season. There is great satisfaction in doing something yourself, doing it right, and seeing the results. The other important lesson was in realizing how much those of us who had been on the team knew about wrestling, training, competing, and winning. Sometimes we do not realize what we already know until we teach it to others.

We had to share head gear. Our equipment was old, well used, and mismatched. I wrestled wearing two different sneakers. We practiced in a classroom in our school with a thin, worn-out mat on the floor.

Yet we bonded like no other team I have seen in my life. Many of my teammates became lifelong friends. We were of different ethnic groups, religions, and races. We ate different foods and our parents spoke different languages. None of that mattered. We were wrestlers! And we knew we couldn't be stopped.

⚖

That season, I was undefeated until I had a match against an opponent who had been the New England champion the previous year.

I made a wrong move and fell, and he tried to pin me. I fought back to keep my other shoulder from being pinned to the mat. It was the longest two minutes of my life. I did not get pinned, but he beat me. I was so exhausted after that match that they had to carry me off the mat.

During the rest of the season, I won every match and was the wrestler to beat in the 138-pound weight class. It was the greatest feeling to walk onto the mat and see Tup, often in his milk delivery uniform, sitting with the other parents, cheering me on. From the audience, I could hear his distinct voice, with his Italian accent, above all the others that were cheering. And I could feel his hand on my shoulder, guiding me to victory match after match.

During the regular season there was one match that stands out. We were wrestling at a private school, and I was distracted because my father, who was a regular fixture at all my wrestling matches, had not shown up yet. He had to work, but he always made a point to show up at every match, fitting it in around his delivery schedule. That day, the 125-pound match was finished, and the officials were now calling the 133-pound match, but Dad still hadn't shown.

I was getting worried that something had happened to him when I heard these jangly chains. I turned around. It was my dad, and he was running in with my younger brother, Joe, running behind him. Dad was wearing his milkman uniform, and the two of them were making a racket as they entered. The front pocket of my father's uniform was always filled with coins, the loose change he collected as payment for the milk bottles that he delivered.

That sound was music to my ears. The sight of my father in his pinstriped uniform and hat always filled me with pride and joy. I knew what it took to do his job and the effort he had to put in each day to provide for us. To me, that uniform was symbolic of my father's success, perseverance, and love for my family. I was relieved because he was there.

Suddenly, I heard a wave of laughter coming from the stands. I realized that everyone was looking at my father and brother, laughing at their appearance and the sound my father made as he ran due to the jangling coins and keys.

I did not like that these private school kids and their privileged families were laughing at my father and brother. They did not deserve to be made into objects of ridicule. Doing so was unnecessary and cruel. What was so funny about a parent arriving to watch his son compete?

Everything that made me so proud of my father was being belittled by these rich folks from the private school. It brought back the memory of my friend's father pointing at me when I delivered milk to their home as a youngster. It stung.

I didn't have time to react before the officials called my weight class. My opponent took off his sweatshirt, and he was all muscle. People started to whoop and cheer at the sight of him and were feeling sorry for me because they thought that this kid was going to wipe the floor with me.

But here is what they hadn't counted on. I was so furious about the way my father was being treated that I channeled it into the match. When the referee blew the whistle, I came out like a wild man. I went after this kid like it was life or death and, and in wrestling terms, I took him down. And I must confess that I heard him grunt as he hit the mat.

When the referee held my arm in the air as the winner of the match, the parents and their children sitting in the stands were not laughing anymore.

My teammates cheered me on, and my father and brother hugged me. What's great about wrestling is that it doesn't matter how much money your parents have, how fancy your home is, how exclusive your school is, or how expensive your equipment and uniforms are. It's a one-on-one competition, and that day I won.

As good as I felt for winning, I still felt bad for my father. It was, at the same time, one of the best and one of the worst experiences I had wrestling.

The lesson here isn't "don't get angry," because we all get angry. We are all frustrated. And everyone has the experience of someone making fun of them or someone they care about. But the critical question is: What do you do with that anger? Does that anger lead to an arrest, a conviction, a prison sentence? Or can that anger be put to good use? Can that anger be a motivator to accomplish something that others think you cannot do?

That's the challenge I am putting to you. Use your anger. Do not let your anger take you down.

At the end of the season, we made it to the state wrestling championship, held at Brown University. Our whole team brought their A game.

My first match, I wrestled a kid who was the Providence County champion. I pinned him in twenty-eight seconds. The next match was against a pretty good wrestler from one of the high schools I had beaten before. I pinned him in a couple of minutes. Those matches were over quickly, and I still had some strength left.

My final match, the match for state champion in the 138-pound weight class, turned out to be between me and that same wrestler who had been the New England champion. He had been wrestling

Wrestling for the high school state championship

Rhode Island State Champion wrestling team

at the 147-pound weight class but, wanting to block our championship hopes, they sweated him down to 138 pounds.

This was the same wrestler who had almost pinned me earlier in the season. He was eager for the rematch, fully intending to come right at me and put me away. He was going to put all his energy into taking me down.

However, as I mentioned, since we coached ourselves, we also spent a good amount of time studying our opponents and crafting a strategy to defeat them.

The ref blew his whistle to start the match, and my opponent came charging at me like he was a two-ton steamroller. But I knew he was going to do that. I was prepared.

I set him up to blow past me, and he fell forward. And then I did the move I had been practicing for weeks to roll him over and pin him. He was stunned. He couldn't understand what had happened. But I had planned it, and it worked. I won the round but couldn't pin him.

In the second period he had a great roll to try and take me down. But I stepped out of the roll and outmaneuvered him, and I was able to win the second period, the match, and the championship. I was lucky to beat him. I was now the Rhode Island State Champion.

And my father was right there, at the side of the mat, to see it all. He gave me a big hug.

CHAPTER 9

My Two-Year Gap

When I was growing up, I didn't personally know any-one who had gone to college—not one of my relatives, friends' parents, or friends' brothers, sisters, or relatives. Having their child go to college was the dream of every parent on Federal Hill. I know it was for my parents. And I knew it was for me. I was the second person in my family to graduate high school out of forty-five cousins, and I was the first to attend college. It was a major accomplishment. It was not just a victory for me but a great victory for my entire family. I was somewhat of a mini celebrity as word spread that I was going to college. It was a really big deal.

After high school I went to Providence College, a Catholic liberal arts college founded by Dominican friars in 1917. Providence College was only a few miles from my home but, for me, it was a different world. I continued to live at home but immensely enjoyed the college environment, and I did my best to absorb as much as I could while on campus. I learned as much outside the classroom as

I did inside. Interacting with classmates from around the country, from all walks of life, was a fascinating experience. It reinforced what my parents had always taught me: hard work, perseverance, and honesty can overcome anything. I realized that many of my classmates may have had more comfortable surroundings and material belongings than I had. But that didn't make them better than me. I had a bumpier road to get there, but I had earned my spot on the field. Plus, I had my mother's home cooked meals every night! There was no stopping me.

During my senior year of college, I applied to Boston University Law School. It was my dream and the culmination of so much determination and hard work. But I wasn't sure if I would be admitted. So, my father and I made an appointment with the dean there to discuss whether I would be accepted to the law school.

My father and I drove to Boston for the interview. My father was extremely nervous, which in turn made me even more nervous. It was understandable that he was nervous. His son's future was about to be decided. And, after all, it was a long way from getting off the ship *Venezia* at the Port of Providence to the office of the Dean of Admissions at BU Law School. As tough and smart as my father was, I sensed for the first time that he was a bit intimidated.

During the interview, it became clear to the dean that my father was so eager to make our case, it was impossible for me to get a word in. He patiently let my father go on for some time and then asked if he could meet with me alone.

After my father had excused himself from our meeting, the dean looked at me and said, "So I know your father wants you to come here to law school. How about you?"

l told him that it was my dream since childhood to go to law school and become a lawyer. That I was the first to go to college in my large extended family. I spoke to him candidly about all my life experiences that I felt were relevant. I even told him about my father's hand on my shoulder.

The dean called my father back into the room and said to us, "Your son will be admitted to law school." I knew law school was going to be expensive, and that I would need to get a job to make it all work, but I could attend. I was overjoyed to be admitted.

On the fifty-mile trek back to Providence, my father was singing Italian songs. He was so happy and proud. I didn't want the ride to end. We were both giddy with excitement.

When we came back home, my mother cooked a big meal, and we celebrated. It was very exciting. It felt like I had just been drafted to a professional sports team in the first round. All our lives would be better. A lawyer in the family would bring credibility, prestige, the ability to really help people, and, finally, some financial security. The next step was to set about the task of finding a job in the Boston area to work at night and on the weekends.

After a few weeks, it became clear to me that I was not going to be able to afford law school. I could maybe cover the cost of tuition, but when it came to room, board, and books, the reality was not that I did not have enough money. In fact, I had no money. There was no financial aid or scholarships available. There was no rich relative from whom to borrow the money. I had the ability and the determination, but I just couldn't afford to move to Boston.

My parents did not have money and couldn't help. Beyond that, I neither wanted to be a burden to them, nor did I want them to think that their circumstances were impacting my ability to attend law school in any way. It was terrible, as I felt I was a disappointment to everyone who had encouraged and helped me get to this point. Especially my parents. I couldn't bear to tell them that their dream for me to be a lawyer was not going to happen.

I decided that what made the most sense for me was to work for a year or two and save up money. I knew I could teach high school during the day and continue to live at home, and when I could afford to, I would go to law school at night—not at Boston University, which did not have a night program, but at Suffolk Law School in Boston, which did.

However, to be a teacher in the Providence public schools, I needed to take the required education courses to get my teaching certificate. To make this plan a reality, I now had to consult Father Quinn, one of the deans at Providence College. I needed his help to get enough credits to qualify as a teacher.

Father Quinn came from an old Boston Brahmin family who were very wealthy. At one point they owned the Boston Braves baseball team. I could not imagine him having any understanding of the problems I faced. Father Quinn was also known to be tough. I was scared to see him because I was convinced this priest was not going to want to help me. I was afraid that all he would see when we met was a poor Italian kid from Federal Hill.

Once I had made the decision to work as a teacher and to go to law school at night, I had to tell my parents I was not going to Boston University Law School. I was worried about how to let my family know. I didn't want my parents to think that they played any role in my decision or were inadequate in any way.

I went home for lunch. My mother sat with me, and I turned to her and said, "I'm really burned out. I've been in school for some sixteen years. I want to take a break for a year."

She was immediately concerned. "What do you mean you want to take a break for a year?"

"I'm just tired," I said. "What I'm going to do is teach and, after a year, I'll go to law school at night."

"You can't do that," my mother instantly said. "You can't do that." She was concerned that once I started getting a paycheck, I would lose interest in going to law school.

"Wait a minute," she said, before running into her bedroom. I could hear her rustling though her drawers. When she returned to the kitchen table, she had three bank books in her hands. They were somewhat tattered and held together by an elastic. She clutched them tightly in her hand and her voice got very serious.

"Dad never made much money," she told me. "But never a week went by that I didn't put something away in a bank. I want you to take these."

I looked through them. Sure enough, every week there was a deposit. Most of them were around fifty cents, maybe a dollar. I think the biggest deposit was three dollars.

Over twenty years she had saved up a little bit more than $2,000. I was thinking of all those years that my mom deprived herself of everything—she never bought herself a new dress, or allowed herself to indulge in some canned peaches she was craving. She always put everyone else first, and she never complained. I teared up as I realized that she wanted to give all of it to me. Those bank books represented a lifetime of hard work and planning for the future. Two thousand dollars was a lot of money in the 1950s, when minimum wage was about a dollar per hour.

I looked at her and said, "I can't take this." At this point, she began to plead with me. We both started to cry. I had visions of her walking down Atwells Avenue every week, going to the bank, and bit by bit tucking any spare cent away, never once thinking of spending any money on herself. I just could not take it. But I promised myself there and then that if Father Quinn helped me get a job teaching and I was able to make enough money, I would go to law school at night.

When I met Father Quinn, his face was quite serious, and he had a stern demeanor. The more I talked, the more fearful I became. I finally laid out my case and sat silently for a few moments waiting for him to respond.

At this point, I had thoroughly convinced myself that I had blown my last possibility and that my plan was not going to work. My dream was over.

Finally, he looked right at me and said, "I think I can help you, but there's a condition attached."

I was curious. "Anything, Father. What do I have to do?" I asked.

"My one condition for helping you is that you promise me that you will follow through and go to law school. Because once you get that first paycheck as a teacher, you may change your mind. I need your word you will see this through and become an attorney."

I promised. And he did help me. Not only did he help me, but he also went above and beyond. He was just a great guy with great understanding. Simply put, I had misread him. I had incorrectly assumed he would never understand my situation. It turned out that he understood it more than I could ever imagine.

At Providence College, I majored in political science, and many of my courses were in history. So, when it came to teaching high school, I was qualified to teach English and social studies. The last thing I had to do to get a teaching job was get approved by the school committee.

I went to my local school committee representative, who told me that he would make an appointment for me to meet with Dr. Handley, the superintendent of schools. "I will recommend you," he said, "but you need to make a good impression on the superintendent."

Dr. Handley's office was in the Department of Education building. I went there to meet with him. I told Dr. Handley what I told Father Quinn, that I wanted to be a lawyer but could not afford to attend, and that I wanted to teach in the day and go to law school at night.

He looked at me and said, "I was supposed to do that. I was supposed to be a lawyer. Then I went into education, and I started making money, and I didn't go to law school." Dr. Handley then said to me exactly what Father Quinn and my mother had told me: "You have to stick to your plan and go to law school." He handed me an application to be a teacher and told me to fill it out right there on the spot. I did, and he told me, "I'm leaving this application right here on my desk. Tomorrow morning, I'll give it to my aides. The school committee is meeting this week and we'll vote on it."

I felt a sense of relief that I was going to be approved as a teacher, which meant that I would also be attending law school, albeit at night, and commuting to Boston. Everything seemed to be in order. I was ready to go!

Later that day when I was driving my car, I saw all these firetrucks with their sirens blaring, rushing at full speed, one after another to what must be a big blaze. I followed them, driving as far as I could until I saw the blaze. The superintendent's building had gone up in flames—and I realized that my application was on his desk! Remember: this was a time before computers, scanning of documents, or copies saved in the cloud. Email didn't exist yet. The paper copy was it!

I realized no application meant no submission to the committee, no approval, no job as a teacher. It was like a scene from a bad movie. I felt helpless. I was panicked.

The next day, I called everyone I could to connect with the superintendent. But no one was in their offices: everything was burned to the ground. I found out that the Department of Education had set up temporary headquarters on the premises of Central High School. That was my alma mater and only a few minutes from my home, so I rushed over there.

When I arrived, there was a police barrier, and they weren't letting anyone in. I told the officer I was there to see the superintendent. I said he would remember me. The officers said, "He can't see you."

"He has to see me," I said. "Tell him it's the person he met with yesterday, whose application to be a teacher was on his desk." The officer promised to see what he could do. He disappeared.

I waited for four hours. Finally, my patience paid off. A different officer came up to me and said, "You can go see the superintendent." I walked into his office, and before I said a word, the superintendent handed me a form and said, "Fill out this application." I was about to say something, but he said, "I know why you're here. Fill out the application." So I did. And later that week I was approved as a teacher.

What I learned from my experiences with people like Father Quinn and Dr. Handley was to never assume what someone will or won't do. Sometimes it's a matter of asking the right person. Sometimes it's timing, and, more often than you think, sometimes people are waiting for the opportunity to help others. Even amid his own emergency, Dr. Handley was willing to help me out.

What stayed with me, as a teacher, a lawyer, a judge—as a person—is that what may seem unimportant to you could be incredibly important and life-changing to the person before you. Whether it is your student, a client, or a person with a parking ticket, one small act of kindness, one act of being thoughtful, can really change the course of a person's life.

And sometimes, even when it looks like everything is against you, even acts of God, persistence can pay off. Don't give up when it gets hard. Dig deep and keep going!

CHAPTER 10

Asking for Help Is the First Step to Getting Help

I ended up teaching civics and history at Hope High School in Providence. After two years, I continued to teach while attending Suffolk Law School at night for the next four years. It took longer than I had planned, but I adjusted and found a way to make my dream happen.

I also really enjoyed teaching. I was only a few years older than the seniors and I could relate well to many of them. During that time, I truly learned as much or more from my students as they did from me.

There was a young man, Robert, in my history class who always sat in the front row with a big smile on his face. He was only getting a 55 average in the class and had flunked history the year before. I wasn't sure why. He was a smart person. However, he was a senior now, and if he flunked history again, he wasn't going to graduate.

So, I called him into my classroom after school one day and told him that I wanted him to write a 2,000-word thesis on the Panama Canal. I told him that I didn't care if it was the best essay ever; it just needed to be in his handwriting and it had to be 2,000 words long. And if he did that, I would pass him.

A week went by, and I received nothing from him, so I pulled him aside again and asked, "Where is your essay?"

"I didn't have time to do it," he answered.

I wasn't happy to do so, but I let him know that I didn't have any choice but to flunk him.

Two days later, I attended a function at the Biltmore Hotel in Providence. While sitting in the ballroom, I saw a face I recognized back in the kitchen.

I flagged down the waiter. "Is that Robert?"

The waiter replied, "Yes, it is."

"Is he working here?" I asked.

"He works here every night," the waiter said. "He comes from a large family, and he has to help support them."

The next morning, I called Robert into my classroom and asked, "Why didn't you tell me you were working?"

Robert answered, "I didn't want to complain."

I had great compassion for Robert. Sometimes you are afraid to share your situation with a teacher or a superior for fear they will think less of you. But, in my experience, if you are honest and transparent, you and whoever you talk with will find a way for you to work out the problem.

Robert and I talked it out and found a way for him to pass my class and graduate.

It's important for teachers to understand how tough some students have it. To the teachers of the world, I would like to ask them all to remember that every student is one great teacher away from becoming a success story. Children need champions. Please be their champion.

As for students, remember this thing about teachers—or priests, or rabbis, or imams, or, for that matter, judges: they see such a wide range of the human experience, and so often at low points or periods of grave trouble. What this means is that their insight into human nature is often much wider and greater than anyone imagines.

So, do not assume what someone else will or won't understand. Try to adopt a mindset of curiosity. When you engage with someone by sharing your own vulnerabilities, desires, hopes, and dreams, it may surprise you that often people will want to help if they can. Give someone the opportunity to make an impression on you by going above and beyond what you ever imagined.

In my courtroom, I saw people from all walks of life. Many of them imagined that my life was nothing like theirs, and that because I was not their age or did not share their ethnicity or their religion, or just because I was a judge, I couldn't understand them, much less their problems. Many times, they've learned that we have a lot more in common than they could have imagined. I hope that at some future date, a person in a position of influence will share how a judge in Providence Municipal Traffic Court understood them and had a positive impact on their life—the same way a judge once had on my own father and grandfather.

CHAPTER 11

Dealing with Prejudice

When I was in college, one of my part-time jobs was working in a restaurant downtown. Valentine, a young woman who worked in a nearby office, would stop in the restaurant, and we struck up a friendship. One day, I summoned the courage to ask her out for a date. She agreed.

I thought I was a hotshot. And a definite catch for any young woman and her family. I was in college. I had a job. I had ambitions to go to law school. I walked and talked with respectful confidence. I had overcome so many obstacles along the way and felt that I had left them far behind.

On the day of the date, I went to her house to pick her up. She lived in a different section of Providence. I was a clean-cut, articulate, and polite young man. Her father was there to greet me and immediately asked, "Where do you live?"

Unfortunately, I saw it coming from a mile away. By the tone in his voice when he said hello, I knew he wasn't happy. I had tried to be vague enough in my answers, but there was no escape from where his questions were pointing.

"Providence," I answered.

"Where in Providence?"

"Bradford Street," I replied.

"On Federal Hill?"

"Yes," I answered. I was too proud to lie about where I was from.

That was all he needed to hear (although I feel he already knew). The next thing he uttered was, "You are not taking out my daughter." And his daughter, who was standing there, started to cry.

"I'm sorry," was all I could say, and walked out. I felt bad for myself and terrible for Valentine. Her father's prejudice was overriding his daughter's judgment, independence, and freedom. Why would Valentine ever confide in her father after that?

I never talked to Valentine about that day. I wish it was the only time I was treated that way. But it wasn't. Throughout my political and professional life, being an Italian from Federal Hill subjected me to unwarranted, undeserved stereotypes by ignorant, shallow, cruel people.

I had thought I had overcome so much: being the first in my family to go to college, having a respectable job, asking out a pretty girl for a date who said yes. Going to a different neighborhood, all excited. I could only imagine endless possibilities.

But I learned that to some people, I could never leave my neighborhood behind. That its reputation had followed me into this young woman's house. For some people, prejudice never goes away.

Unfortunately, it was a lesson I would have to learn over and over again—even from people I thought were my friends.

When I first finished college, I was a high school civics teacher during the day and coached the wrestling team after school. At night, I drove fifty miles to Boston for law school. After classes, I drove back to Providence. I would get home around 11 PM and get started on my law school homework and my lesson plans for the classroom. That was my daily routine, and it was grueling.

When I got home, my mother would be cooking, and my father would be sitting at the table. I'd say, "Mom, I'm not hungry. You don't have to cook." And she'd say, "Dad's hungry. He wants me to cook something for him." That was how it went every night.

One day I was driving to Boston when, halfway there, my car died. I had to leave it in a restaurant parking lot where they said I could come back for it the next day.

I hitchhiked the rest of the way to class. Afterward, I walked to the train station with an older gentleman in our class. He was about to retire from the National Labor Relations board in Boston and wanted to become a labor lawyer.

It was February and freezing outside. So, when we got to the station in Providence, and I realized that he had a car parked there, I said to him, "If you're headed my way, I'd appreciate a lift."

Federal Hill was out of his way, but he offered to drive me home, nonetheless. When we got to our corner, I said, "This is it. You can drop me off right here."

"Where do you live?" he asked incredulously as I was getting out of the car. He was looking around at the houses from the windows of his car. I pointed to the building where I lived right on the corner. It was a clapboard apartment house, a dilapidated tenement, and the exterior was in disrepair. I never really noticed the imperfections on the outside of the building because it was my home.

My family didn't worry about the exterior. We cherished that we were together inside the house. My favorite part of each day was walking in the door and being greeted by my parents and my brothers. My home was a place of sanctuary, filled with encouragement, hope, comfort, safety, and, most importantly, love.

I was already picturing my mother waiting for me upstairs, with my father already at the table. The gentleman in the car looked at the building and then said, "If you want to be a successful lawyer, you can't live in a house like that."

To this day, I cannot understand the insensitivity of making a comment like that to someone. How cruel to say something like that to somebody in my circumstances. The truth was, we were happy to have what we had. But his saying that had a profound impact on me. I still clearly remember it all these years later. I realized that some people have no idea of the impact of what they say.

At the time, I simply replied, "Thank you for the ride." But I never talked to him again. I will never forget how he behaved. I am reminded of one of my favorite quotes by Maya Angelou: "I've learned that people will forget what you said, people will forget what you did, but people will never forget how you made them feel."

Since that experience, I try hard to always consider a person's situation when talking to them.

CHAPTER 12

The World's Greatest Mom

When I was teaching high school, I had several students who made an impression on me. One of them was a young woman, Joyce Tibaldi. She was intelligent and had a great personality. Her grandparents were Italian immigrants, and her parents were first-generation Americans. Her father worked in a factory. Unfortunately, he died young, in his fifties. She had an older brother, also named Frank, and a younger brother, Charles. Her brother Frank Tibaldi eventually became the traffic engineer for the City of Providence; Charles Tibaldi, who was a star football player at Boston University, became an attorney.

Several years later when I met Joyce again, she was an attractive young woman, and we began to date. However, those were the years when I barely had a minute to myself. Not only was I still teaching high school, but I was also going to law school three nights a week in Boston. I was in the National Guard, and I had training on Thursdays and one weekend a month. I had also won a seat on the city council. My teaching job paid $3,800 a year and the city council position paid an additional $1,200. That was barely enough to pay my law school tuition and live on, much less be able to start a family. However, once I started dating Joyce, there was never any doubt in my mind that we were going to marry. I knew I just had to persevere to reach my goals—all of them.

Joyce was very patient with me. We finally married after dating for five years, and then two years later we had our first child, Frank Jr. Over the next seven years, we were blessed with four more children: David, John, Marissa, and Paul. It might sound clichéd, but meeting Joyce and having our children truly taught me about the power of love. When you find the right person, you are full of love for them. And when you have children, you do not split your love between them—you love all your children 100 percent. Somehow your heart expands, opening itself in ways you never imagined.

Our wedding

It is both a blessing and a miracle—and yet, at the same time, it is the most natural thing. It happens all by itself.

Joyce was the world's greatest mom. She was in charge of making sure that the kids got to school and to their after-school activities, that we were all fed and had clean clothes, and that our house was in order. She did this all by herself without any hired help. I helped as best I could, but it was Joyce who was really in charge of the day-to-day. If I admire women so greatly it is because of the examples set by my grandmother, mother, and Joyce.

Anyone who has been married for many years and has children knows that it is not always easy. You are so focused on your children and their welfare that it is easy to forget about your spouse. Many couples divorce after their children are out of the house, finding that raising their children was the glue that kept their relationship

My family

together. Joyce and I understood the importance of raising our children but also the strength of our bond. Respect, compassion, and understanding are important in all things, and particularly so in a marriage.

Joyce and I have been married for more than sixty years. That puts us into a very small group—some estimate that only about 7 percent of the population have marriages that last that long. I believe that the secret to a long and successful marriage is not just finding someone you can live with for fifty years—it's finding someone you can't live without.

Joyce is incredible, and I appreciate everything she does. As best I can, I let her know. Nowadays, Joyce dotes on our seven grandchildren and two great-grandchildren and also presides over the Sunday dinners in our family, much as my own mother once did.

CHAPTER 13

We Can't Choose Family

There is an old saying that we can choose our friends, but we can't choose our family.

I understand that sometimes a family member's behavior is so toxic that you need to put space between yourself and them. Often, family members are as different as day and night, but that doesn't mean you can't come to appreciate them for who they are. This has been particularly true in my family.

When I first ran for the Providence City Council, I was the underdog by a long measure. No one thought I had a chance at winning, other than me and my father. The first couple of months after we opened my campaign headquarters, my father would sit there just so it looked like there were people working.

My problem was that the councilman I was running against was very powerful. He was responsible for a lot of people on Federal

Hill having city jobs. Everyone was scared to death to even be seen in my headquarters.

Besides my father, my Uncle Pari came every day. Today we would have recognized him as a special needs person. He was sort of a tough guy and a hard worker. But he had an unpredictable side and often flew off the handle.

He was also a man of many nicknames. Some called him Santa Claus, and still others called him Hot Stuff. There's a story behind each of those nicknames.

Take Santa Claus: My grandparents lived near the railroad tracks. My grandfather had died, and my grandmother was working

Celebrating my upset victory to the Providence City Council in 1962. Tup is pictured at the bottom left, Uncle William behind Tup, Uncle "Pippy" to the right of William, cousin Billy to my right, and younger brother Joe to my left.

the fruit cart, and Pari worked on the cart as well. He collected the money. Over time, Pari and my grandmother were able to put some extra money aside, maybe $100. Now, Pari loved to dance, so he wanted to go dance down at a local ballroom. He went out and bought a red suit using the money that they'd saved and went dancing.

My grandmother found out. She wanted to know where the money went, and when she found out Pari took the money, she went on the attack.

While Pari was sleeping in bed, she got a broomstick and went after him with it. Because he lived on the first floor, he threw on some clothes and jumped out the window. He ran down to the railroad tracks and jumped on the first freight train that went by, which happened to be headed for New York.

He stayed in New York for two years until he came back for Christmas and my grandmother forgave him. That's why he was called Santa Claus.

As for Hot Stuff? At union meetings, everyone would tell Uncle Pari their gripes; riled up and not caring who he offended, Uncle Pari would scream at the union leaders, telling them, "You're a bunch of bums. You're crooks. All you're interested in is yourself." He had a temper and was known to be volatile. Anything could set him off. So, people called him Hot Stuff and Santa Claus, depending on the day.

Pari worked for the public school department of the City of Providence as part of their painting crew. He worked hard, but he did not get along with his boss. There were a lot of people with whom he didn't get along. He held grudges against all sorts of people for long periods of time.

Pari used to say to me, "If you get elected, I want you to fire [my boss] and make me the boss of painters." I thought he was kidding. He was close to sixty years old, could not read, and had trouble talking. There was no world where he could be the boss of painters.

However, against all odds, I won that election. And, always persistent, Pari immediately asked me if he was now going to be boss of painters. I told him I would see what could be done.

The next time I met with the mayor, he asked how things were going in the district and if there was anything he needed to address. We discussed several issues, and near the end of the meeting, I mentioned that Pari didn't get along with his boss.

The mayor told me that the boss of painters was a friend of his, but Pari could easily be transferred. In fact, with his seniority, he could oversee painting public schools, which was both a promotion and put him on equal footing with his enemy, the boss of painters. This was normal politics and perfectly acceptable at the time. To the winner went the jobs.

I was overjoyed. I went to see Pari to tell him the good news.

He did not see it that way. Anything less than his boss being fired was unacceptable. "You sold me out to the mayor," he said. "You're a sellout."

Pari went into a rage. He stopped talking to me. He couldn't stand that his boss still had his job.

Time goes by, and eventually I was running for reelection. Winning the first time might have been a fluke, but this time my opponents were coming for me.

Pari was still so angry that he decided to run against me for City Council and have his candidacy help my opponents. His whole campaign was based on calling me a sellout.

One of my opponent's headquarters was about two blocks from mine on Atwells Avenue. My Aunt Angie, who was one of my father's sisters who had taken care of Pari over the years, and who was one tough woman, came to my headquarters when she saw Pari working in my opponent's campaign office. She wanted to make sure I knew and that she was going to take care of it.

She then went to the opponent's headquarters and said, "Pari, what are you doing? You're betraying our family. We got a nephew, finally something good happens in this family, and this is what you do?" The story goes that she then grabbed him and started shaking him. Naturally, he began to resist her assault.

At that moment, somebody walked by and saw my Aunt Angie and Uncle Pari and assumed he was beating up Angie. They called the police.

Meanwhile, I was speaking at a rally about three blocks away when someone ran up and whispered to me, "They're beating up Angie at your opponent's headquarters." At this point, a bunch of my campaign staff rushed over. And a giant fight broke out.

As soon as I could break free, I rushed out to join my campaign staff at the opponent's headquarters. It took me about three minutes to get there. When I arrived, the scene before me was crazy. The cops were there. They arrested everybody and brought them all down to the station.

Everybody eventually got released. Fortunately, they did not charge anybody. But there was a big article in the paper with the headline "Family Feud."

Although Pari ran against me, I ended up winning the reelection, and I won big. But that is not the end of the story.

Three years went by. By then I was married to Joyce, and we were living in a house off Broadway right in the heart of Federal Hill. It was a Sunday afternoon. We were out and had a babysitter at home with our first child, my son Frankie. When we arrived home, the babysitter had a look of horror on her face. This was before the age of smart phones, so there had been no way for her to reach us.

"What's the matter?" I immediately asked.

"There's some guy in the house," she said. "And he says his name is Santa Claus."

"Santa Claus?" I asked. She said yes.

I went into the big room across from our kitchen to find Pari on the sofa, sound asleep. I still remember it was pouring outside that day. I sat in my chair a few feet away from him and started to watch television, knowing at some point he would wake up. Suddenly, I saw him stir.

"Uncle Pari, how are you?" I asked.

He looked up at me without blinking and said, "Frankie. Frankie."

"Yeah, Uncle Pari?"

"Can you let me borrow $300?"

I knew there was no way I would ever see that $300 again if I were to lend it to him. And despite not seeing him in three years, I knew from our extended family that he had his daughter's financial support as well. But something in me made me say, "Yeah, I can handle that, Uncle Pari. I'll give that to you." Never a word about anything that had happened a few years prior.

I gave him $300.

"Okay, I'm going to go now," he said.

"Wait a minute," I said. "It's pouring outside. I'll give you a ride."

"You sure?" he said. "I can walk."

He lived about five blocks away. So, I drove him home, and we resumed being friendly after that. My Uncle Santa Claus Hot Stuff.

The lesson here is that in every family, sometimes bad behavior occurs. But what are you going to do? They're family.

When people tell me stories about their families, all I can say is, "It's all relative."

CHAPTER 14

A PhD in Human Nature

The majority of my many uncles and cousins were trades-people. Few of them or their spouses even graduated high school. My whole childhood, I was in and out of their houses, and they were in ours. There was no problem they did not experience, and no problem that they didn't solve together.

In their lives, I saw all of humanity—and years later, when I became a judge, I understood the experiences of the people who came before me in court because of my grandparents, parents, uncles, aunts, and cousins. Whatever their circumstance, I have seen it and lived it either personally or vicariously through one of my family.

Amadeo, my mother's first cousin whom everyone called Her-bie, stood at my baptism as my godfather. As far back as I could remember, he'd come to visit me every Christmas Eve. When he came to visit, he would give me a silver dollar.

I only saw him once a year, but when I did, it was special. He never missed showing up. He would come in, and he would hug my mother and my dad, then call to me, "My godson!" He made me feel very special.

When I was sixteen years old, my godfather showed up as always for his Christmas Eve visit. But this time he looked at me and said, "I've come to visit you for sixteen years, every Christmas. Now, since you're going to be driving next year, you will come and see me." And I did. Every year since, I'd visit him on Christmas Eve. And each year, I would have to bring him a present.

Years went by. I was a married man and had my first child. I brought him with me to visit my godfather on Christmas Eve. And the same was true for the next child, and the next. And before you know it, I was going to see him with all five of my children.

By now, his daughter was married to the son of a doctor, and that was a big deal for him. They all lived together in a house where his daughter and son-in-law had the upstairs apartment, and he was in the downstairs basement, which had its own kitchen.

He was such an unbelievable cook. Christmas Eve was celebrated with the Feast of the Seven Fishes, and he would be cooking the feast for his family. I'd bring my kids, and they would eat half the food!

Finally, one Christmas Eve, I had another obligation. By then I had my legal practice, I was a Providence city councilman, and I had my own five children. I was too tired to make two stops that night, so I thought to myself, "I'll go see him tomorrow." For fifty-five years we had not missed one night, so I figured it would be all right if I went by his house on Christmas Day this one time.

The next day, I went to his house with a present. I rang the doorbell, and his wife answered.

"Mary," I said, "how are you?"

She said, "Thank God you're here."

"What's the matter?" I said.

She replied, "All night he's been saying, 'I wonder what happened to Frankie? When I saw him last time, did I say something to insult him? Did anybody say anything?' He said, 'I can't believe this, after all these years we broke this off. This was such a wonderful thing.'"

She told me he was in the other room. "He's really sulking."

I walked in. "*Padrone.*" Godfather, I called him. "How are you doing?"

He said, "Good."

I gave him the gift I brought. He turned to me and said, "How's everything?"

"Everything is great," I said, adding, "I'm very sorry I couldn't make it yesterday."

"I knew you'd be here," he said. "That's why I'm waiting."

He forgave me, but from then on, until the day he died, I never missed another Christmas Eve. I must have gone for some sixty-five years.

My godfather, in his way, taught me a great deal. He taught me respect. And in such a simple way: "I respected you. I came here every Christmas Eve. Now it's your turn." And then the one time I missed going to him, his simple comment of "I knew you'd be here. That's why I'm waiting" was all the reprimand I needed. He did not shame me; he just set me straight in a respectful way. Showing me how it was done.

What he was teaching me were old country values of honor and respect that you must learn through example.

Children learn what they live. If they live in a home where respect is expected and given, they will take that code of conduct into adulthood, where it will become a helpful tool as they strive to become happy, successful, and contributing members of their communities.

CHAPTER 15

How Prejudice Affected My Political Career

After serving on the Providence City Council for eight years, I decided to run for statewide office. I had big political aspirations, and in 1970, I decided to run for attorney general of Rhode Island.

One of the advisers warned me, "You know, Frank, you better be careful because you're from Federal Hill, Italian, and the son of immigrants. You're running for Rhode Island Attorney General, and you're going to get accused of being involved with organized crime."

"How can that be?" I said. "Number one, my life is all documented. I worked in the restaurant. I worked shining shoes. I worked delivering papers. I did all of this to pay my own way through college.

After college, I couldn't afford to go to a law school, so I was a public school teacher to support myself, to support my family. How can anyone say I have ties to organized crime? That'll never stick."

Sadly, I was wrong about that.

The last week of the campaign, I was ahead in the polls when the Republicans, along with the Republican candidate for governor and the Republican candidate for attorney general, had a political parade on Federal Hill. As the parade went by, a group of women and a few men, all holding Caprio signs, decided to taunt those marching. They screamed at the candidates, "You bums!" as they marched past.

The next day, headlines on the front page of the *Providence Journal* proclaimed, "Caprio supporters attack governor's parade and attorney general's parade." The article made it seem like the group had shot them. Immediately, the rumors began like wildfire: it was the Mafia; it was organized crime; they're supporting Caprio; he's tied up with them.

In the days running up to the election, the *Providence Journal*, the most important newspaper in Rhode Island and, historically, not a fan of Italians, quoted my opponent as saying that I had shown "an utter indifference to the problem of organized crime" and noted "that such criminal activity has been operating out of Mr. Caprio's own Federal Hill."

It was terribly unfair to insinuate these things about me. Everyone who knew me understood that I was the child of immigrants and self-made. Everybody knew my father, Tup, and they knew what sort of a person he was. My brother Anthony was a policeman at that time. To say that we had anything to do with organized crime was to negate all our hard work and everything we were proud to achieve.

I contacted the *Journal* to say that I was deeply hurt and offended by the innuendo of my opponent. "It had absolutely no basis . . . it's outrageous," I said. But the damage was done. The last thing the people in Rhode Island would vote for was an attorney general who was perceived to have ties to organized crime.

It took me a long, long time to let that go. If I'm being honest, I'm not sure I'm over it still. It's not something I like to discuss because it reopens deep wounds.

Being the victim of such a vicious, unfounded smear campaign could have made me a bitter and intolerant person. Easily. But it did not. I understand it is my choice whether I let things consume me or let them go. Most days, I let them go. And in my courtroom, I worked hard not to make judgments about other people based on innuendo or prejudices, because I have been through that.

Making assumptions and believing generalizations about a specific person based on their ethnicity, race, country of origin, or even their appearance is a lazy way of thinking. It is often a barrier to really seeing the person before you. It's not easy to rid yourself of those biases and prejudices that you may have grown up with or seen or heard from your friends and in the media. But we must all strive to see each person as an individual, not as a stereotype.

CHAPTER 16

Becoming a Judge

The rewards and satisfaction of mentoring others, most agree, is as great or greater for the mentor. Sometimes, when you least expect it, that kindness is paid back in ways you never imagined. And, in no small part, that was how I became a judge.

Let me explain: many years after I had served many terms on the Providence City Council, Joseph Paolino, who came from a prominent Providence family, ran for the seat I originally held.

I advised him and took him under my wing, and we became very friendly. We developed a very strong bond that we maintain to this day. Joe went on to become city council president and then mayor. President Clinton then appointed him U.S. ambassador to Malta. I couldn't have been happier for him or prouder of his accomplishments.

One day, while he was mayor, I got a call from Joe. I was having lunch, and I was called away from the table by a waiter who said, "The mayor is calling you."

I was always happy to hear from Joe. He told me he had some exciting news he wanted to share with me. I assumed it was going to be about something he had done, or something that Providence had achieved or was going to receive.

Instead, what he told me was that one of Providence's three municipal court judges had been appointed to the Rhode Island State Court.

I was happy to hear about it but wasn't sure why he had called me at lunch to tell me about it.

"This creates a vacancy on the municipal court—and I think you should be appointed to the judgeship," Joe said. "I think you'd make a great judge."

I was surprised . . . and delighted. I was honored. Becoming a judge would be the fulfilment of one of my dreams, as well as those of my grandmother and Tup. And being a municipal judge is a part-time position that allows you to continue to have a legal practice, which I needed to do to support my family.

Judges are appointed in Providence not by the mayor but by the city council. It had been almost fifteen years since I'd served on the city council and many of its members were now people with whom I had not served. However, Joe knew them all and promised to call each individually to recommend me. If the mayor recommends someone strongly, there is a good chance the council will listen to him.

The city council voted me in as a judge of the municipal court to finish out the term of the judge I was replacing—and from then on, I would be up for reelection by the city council every four years. I immediately called Tup, who was as proud as he could be. We didn't have to say it, but that hand he had placed on my shoulder had paid off in ways we both never imagined.

Now, you might think there was a big official ceremony for my becoming a judge. But, instead, all I got was a notice from the chief judge in Providence, saying, "You're on the bench next Tuesday." So, my family organized to have one hundred of our family and friends in the courtroom as I was sworn in. And then, later that night, there was a surprise black-tie party my family threw for me. It was a major event in our family—from living in Teano to being an American judge in one generation's time!

From that day on, I never had a better job than being a judge or one that I was prouder to perform. As I travel around the world and am recognized from my court proceedings shown on social media, I often think of the unexpected phone call that I received from Joe in 1985. Joe believed I would make a good judge, just as Tup believed I would make a good lawyer. I am proud that I have lived up to their expectations.

CHAPTER 17

The Best Meatballs

Tup was a strong presence in all my children's lives. My eldest son, Frank Jr., went to Harvard and played on both the football and baseball teams there. Tup never missed a game. In just two generations, Tup had gone from arriving in the US as an immigrant to seeing his grandson play ball for one of America's top universities. That's what makes America great.

Tup had a profound influence on Frank Jr. Unfortunately, he died just before Frank's senior year. That year, when Frank played football, he'd write TUP on white athletic tape and tape his wrists, both for good luck and as a reminder of where he came from. In a way, Tup was right there on the field with him.

One Saturday that year, Frank and the Harvard team were coming to Providence to play Brown. It was a proud day for me, so we invited over a hundred people to the tailgate to celebrate my son's accomplishments with good food, wine, and drinks. This, too, was in honor of Tup.

With my brothers, Anthony (*center*) and Joe

Since Frank's freshman year, my father insisted that we bring enough food to every game so that we could share with the other parents. That was just how his brain worked. Tup would always engage in conversation with the other families at the games and offer them some food. Yet it took my father almost Frank's entire freshman season to convince any of the other families to come to our tailgate and eat with us. Because we were not serving chicken wings and chips. We were serving our best traditional Italian specialties. Slowly he worked on them, and once one family tried some, and the wonderful aroma drifted through the parking lot, the floodgates opened, and Tup would hold court around big platters of Italian food. By the time the game was being played at Brown

University's stadium, there was a regular crew that counted on us for great food during tailgating before the games.

$$\star$$

I asked my Aunt Virginia and Aunt Bianca to make meatballs for the large tailgate party. Among my many aunts, Virginia and Bianca had never married because they had spent their lives taking care of their mother with whom they lived. In many ways, they led sheltered lives. But there was something that they knew better than many college graduates: they knew how to cook. Their meatballs were the best, not just in my opinion but in the opinion of anyone who tasted them.

When I asked them to make meatballs for the party, they worked themselves up into such a tizzy. Aunt Virginia and Aunt Bianca were very proud of my son and wanted to make sure that everything was perfect for all the fancy people that would be at the game. I started getting emergency calls from them: "Frankie, Frankie!" they exclaimed to me. "We don't have big enough pans for all the meatballs."

I went out and bought two big pans for them.

The next call came: "Frankie, Frankie, we don't know how we should make the meatballs. Round, or like we make them? What do the Americans like?"

I told my aunts to make the meatballs as they knew best. To make them as our family loved them—ovals.

Then I got the final, panicked call.

"How do we get to the stadium?" they asked. I told them the street name, which meant nothing to them. "But *how* do we get there?!"

Virginia told me that they had never been to the Brown University campus, which was not far from where they lived, just on the other side of the Providence River. Although they'd lived in Providence their entire lives, they rarely left Federal Hill and had never crossed downtown to the ritzy area on the east side.

I was initially shocked. But after a minute or two, it made absolute sense to me. There was never a reason for them to go to the east side. We had no family there, and everything they needed was a short walk away on Federal Hill.

So, I gave them directions, which they diligently wrote down and repeated to me three times before we hung up. They even took a test ride later that night to make sure the directions were correct.

The day of the game finally came, and these two little ladies, wearing hair nets, were standing in the parking lot of Brown Stadium, ladling out meatballs that they had been cooking all night to whomever came by.

I have to say, they were the tastiest meatballs they ever made. They were always superb, but on this occasion, Virginia and Bianca outdid themselves. People still talk about Aunt Virginia and Aunt Bianca's meatballs. And neither of them ever returned to the east side. If you wanted more meatballs, you had to go to Federal Hill!

The point of this story is simple: everyone has something to contribute to others. And if you are very lucky that something can be very tasty.

CHAPTER 18

Caught in Providence

I have been known to refer to my younger brother, Joe, as "No-filter Joe" because he says whatever is on his mind. He can say the most embarrassing things, and you will always end up laughing along with him. My son Frank Jr. likes to say that if Joe can't make you laugh or get you very upset, you're not alive.

Joe always marched to the tune of his own drummer. Early on, he became obsessed with videography and was one of the early adopters of VHS and eventually of digital technology. In the late 1980s, in the years before the internet, community television became a new enterprise, with cable systems being required to offer community access for local programming. Joe signed up and received the rights to two hours daily of community programming, one segment at two in the afternoon and the other at two in the morning.

To fill his time slot, Joe started filming aspects of life in Providence. He filmed the traffic on Highway 95 and Little League games. However, no matter what he filmed, he never seemed to have enough material. This weighed on Joe so much that at one Sunday night family dinner, Joe said, "I'm desperate for material. Anyone have any suggestions of what I could film?"

It was then that Joyce, my wife, said, "Why don't you film your brother's courtroom? There's plenty going on there."

I said, "No! No way. Absolutely not. I would never do that."

Joyce insisted. I bet you can guess who won that argument.

Irene, Joe's wife, came up with the catchy title, *Caught in Providence.*

My brother Joe filmed my courtroom for twenty-seven years.

As an actual sitting judge, I could neither enter into a contract nor be paid to appear on the program, as that would be a blatant conflict of interest.

People appearing in the courtroom were given the option of appearing on camera or not. Joe's company, CityLife Productions, would shoot, edit, and air the show for no pay, as it was a public access channel.

Over the years, *Caught in Providence* grew from a local Providence community television program to the first show in America to go from a public access station to a network affiliate, the Rhode Island ABC station.

In 2015, my friend John Methia began to post short episodes on YouTube. In 2017, he told us, "There's this new thing on Facebook called Facebook Watch. We should try it out and see how the episodes play outside of Providence."

That same year, the magic call came out of the blue from TV syndication executive Brad Johnson. Brad had seen some of the show's videos and had followed a discussion about it on Reddit. He was impressed that it was an authentic, spontaneous, unscripted court proceeding that had so much heart, compassion, and kindness. He reached out to John, whose company logo, Sociable LLC, appeared on the Facebook posts. Brad worked with Debmar-Mercury, and convinced its owner, Mort Marcus, to watch several of our episodes. Marcus then authorized Brad to tell us that Debmar-Mercury was prepared to syndicate the show nationally.

Caught in Providence, for which Brad remained our senior producer, aired for several seasons on more than 200 stations around the United States, and was nominated for a Daytime Emmy in 2021,

2022, 2023, and 2024. Episodes from my courtroom continue to amass billions of views on social media.

Recently, in 2023, I stepped down from the bench, and Joe decided to end filming my courtroom. But what a ride we had!

Caught in Providence was nominated for the Daytime Emmy Awards in 2021, 2022, 2023, and 2024.

I hope these stories give you a good sense of how I learned the values that informed my life and career and informed how I dispensed justice in my courtroom. I hope to pass along those valuable lessons in the following examples from my courtroom as well as from my business and personal life.

PART TWO

Compassion

I f there is one lesson I could teach, or one quality that I could impart to others, the most important would be *compassion*.

Having compassion is not genetic. It is a learned trait. Compassion is something that is never too late to learn, and never too late to practice. All you need to do is to put yourself in the shoes of the person you are facing and then ask yourself: What would help? How would you behave if it were your parents, grandparents, brother, sister, or relative in that situation?

As someone who was part of a large family, every situation makes me think of something that happened to someone I know, and I ask myself: How would I want them treated?

As I explained at the start of this book, empathy and compassion are often spoken of interchangeably, but they are different. Empathy is when you feel another's pain; compassion is when you feel motivated to do something about it or want to see it changed.

For some people, such as addiction counselors, social workers, and advocates for children and abused women, being compassionate is part of their job. For the rest of us, demonstrating compassion is not always easy. However, the first step is having empathy for that person's plight.

Let me give one example of how seeing another person so full of empathy set an example for me. One day when I was around ten years old, I came home to find my mother sobbing. I said, "Mom, what's the matter?"

She showed me a picture: it was Father Edward J. Flanagan of Boys Town, a nonprofit dedicated to caring for children and families, opening his door to find a child carrying an even smaller child on his back. The words on the photo said simply: "He ain't heavy, he's my brother."

My mother, who at that time was living in a building that probably would never pass a city inspection, felt so much for these little kids in the picture that she was crying her heart out. That was how I learned empathy. And my desire to help those kids, and make my mother feel better, is what taught me compassion.

Compassion comes from never forgetting where you came from and always being grateful for what you have, what you've received, and what you've attained.

Compassion is a good deed we pay forward to others.

Compassion is recognizing that, when we encounter someone who is in any way less fortunate or who faces greater challenges, "There but for the grace of God go I."

Having compassion is what made me successful as a teacher, as an attorney, and as a judge.

The people who came before me in court didn't want to be there. My court handled mostly traffic tickets, not crimes. The people could simply pay their fine and avoid coming to court. In most cases, they couldn't afford the fines, as even a $30 parking ticket could mean that there was no money for groceries that day. They had a job to be at, they had kids to care for, but they were showing up in court at 8 AM because they wanted to resolve their problem, and because they knew that doing so was the right thing to do. How could I not have compassion for them?

CHAPTER 19

My First Day as a Judge Taught Me Much About Compassion

On my first day as a judge, my father was in the courtroom. Having never missed a wrestling match, Tup certainly was not going to miss my first day on the bench! One of my first cases involved a woman who came to court owing several hundred dollars of parking ticket fines.

"Well, I'm just not paying," she told me. "I can't pay. I just don't have the money. I've got kids. I can't pay, and that's it."

I said, "Well, we'll put you on a payment plan," but she was very stubborn and had a lot of attitude. She said, "Well, I'm not going to pay anyway."

I did not like that this woman was so defiant, and it was my job to enforce the law. Maybe I was a little tougher and rougher with her than I should have been. I said, "If you're not going to pay, a boot is going to end up on your car." She continued to say she wasn't going to pay.

"That's it," I said, "No need for any further discussion." I banged my gavel and moved on to the next case.

At the end of the court session, my father came into my chambers. I said, "Dad, how did I do?"

He did not look happy. His brow was furrowed.

"That woman," he said, referring to the woman who didn't want to pay her parking ticket fines. "She has kids."

"Dad," I said, "she was so frustrating. She wouldn't listen. She was disrespectful."

"She was disrespectful," he said, "because she was scared. She was feeling down. She didn't have any money. She's got kids, Frankie," he told me. "You booted her car. How will her kids get to school? How will she shop for groceries for them?"

After my father left that day, I felt depleted, empty. My father made me realize that I needed to think more about the defendant and what was going on in their lives than how they made me feel. Being a judge was about them and their lives, not me. What I thought of as "doing the right thing" caused more harm than it did good. How was that justice?

That was my first day on the bench, and I still think about it. Tup, who didn't get past the eighth grade, taught me more about being a judge that day in my chambers than I learned in four years of law school and twenty-five years as a lawyer. He gave me the most insightful and effective judicial wisdom and quickly set me on the right path. The lesson was that being a judge is much more about the person in front of you than it is about the law.

Since then, I always tried to find out what was really going on with the person, and I always considered how my ruling would impact not only them but their whole family.

CHAPTER 20

The Generosity of Others

I have always believed that laws are not written to break people's spirit or to rob them of an opportunity to get their life back on track. As a judge, I often found myself of two minds: on the one hand, I wanted to impose a just fine on people who had broken the traffic regulations or failed to pay their parking or speeding tickets. What is more, the City of Providence, a place I deeply care for, relied on the revenue it received from these offenders as part of its annual budget. That said, I did not believe my job was to be a revenue generator for the city.

My job as judge was to balance the interests of the city with the rights of the individual, and my natural inclination was to side with the individual.

There were many situations where fining the defendant would have done more harm than good. Making it so a parent can't afford to feed their children is not my idea of justice. Making it so some-one just getting out of jail cannot get a place to live or drive for a job interview is not my idea of justice. Making it so someone's spirit is broken because they had to illegally park to get a veteran to the emergency room as soon as possible is not my idea of jus-tice. How were the ends of justice served if I imposed a maximum penalty on or revoked the license of a parent in financial difficulty who then could no longer take their kids to school or drive to work? In that case, I was compounding problems, not meting out a just punishment.

As I said so often, "Under my robe, I have a heart, not a badge." And if anyone thinks that I was wrong to take a person's situation into consideration when deciding the fine or sentence, I must disagree.

Then, one day, something magical happened, and I was privi-leged to see how one act of kindness can trigger a tsunami of help-ing others.

It began simply: I received a letter from a single mom, Angie Chesser. She was living in Indiana, where she worked in a super-market for minimum wage. She wrote to tell me that she watched the program regularly; and she sent me a check for $20, asking me to use it to help somebody in need.

I read that letter in court when I used those funds, and eventu-ally it was seen on television and on social media. The court began to receive donations, unsolicited, from all over the world, that var-ied from three $1 bills from China to a $1,000 check from a priest. I've seen that a small donation from a stranger can change some-body's life. Often, it provided a soul pump not only for the person receiving the donation but also for the sender!

The letters that accompanied the donations were both heartwarming and heartbreaking, and they gave me a great deal of confidence in the basic goodness of people all over the world. There was a tremendous outpouring of understanding, compassion, and sympathy for the underprivileged—much more than you would think or believe if you only read the newspaper or listened to the radio or the evening news. Importantly, these donations were proof of the power and possibility provided by an army of everyday folks.

I placed these donations in the registry of the court to be used at the court's discretion. For example, if a woman owed $100 on a ticket but I saw that she was in a tough financial situation and all she could pay was $50, I could decide to use $50 from the fund to help her.

That fund became known as the Filomena Fund, named in honor of my mother. The empathy and compassion of so many people reminded me of my mother and her reaction to that photo of Father Flanagan and the two children. Her empathy filled me with compassion for others, so I named the fund after her.

Whenever I used those funds in court, I liked to tell people a little bit about my mom. I would tell them that she was considered one of the best cooks in the neighborhood, and that she was very compassionate, understanding, loving, and sympathetic. She had all the best qualities.

"If she were here," I said, "she'd probably give you a big hug, maybe cook you a meal, and tell you it's going to be okay." Because that is the way she was.

Over the years, in my courtroom, we were able to help many defendants, as you will see in many of the cases described in this book. And it all started with Angie's letter and her donation. One small act of kindness from one woman leading to a wave of people reaching out to help others.

With Angie Chesser

On one memorable morning, I had a young woman before me, Yinka Amandou Mila, who was born and raised in Providence and who was helping to support her niece's four children. She was respectful to the court, but she also had multiple parking violations that she had incurred over time.

She told me that she watched my videos for several years. "Your generosity is unmatched," she said.

I doubt that is the case. However, I told Yinka, "I'm going to tell you something about generosity." That day we had a special visitor in the courtroom: Angie Chesser herself.

I told Yinka about Angie and how her one act of generosity had multiplied and multiplied and touched so many lives.

I asked Angie whether Yinka was the sort of person she had in mind to help when she wrote her letter. Angie agreed she was. Yinka's fines were paid out of the fund, and I asked Yinka to use some of the money saved to buy ice cream for her niece's children.

⚖

Since I retired in 2023 and no longer sit on the bench in Providence Municipal Court, the court can no longer make use of donations for defendants in the courtroom. Instead, the Filomena Fund is now under the umbrella of the Rhode Island Foundation, a community foundation established to serve the people of Rhode Island. Funds received by the Filomena Fund are used to further the charitable work of organizations recognized as 501(c)(3) nonprofits by the IRS, such as Amos House (a food pantry), Providence College, and various veteran's organizations and hospitals, among others.

On more than one occasion, a defendant has made a pledge in the courtroom to donate to a charity, such as Amos House. I never know if they will or not, but I like to give them the benefit of believing they will. After all, my courtroom was full of examples of selfless behavior.

One such case was Donna Morales, who came into my courtroom with her son, Kevante. She was a single mom who had recently lost her job and was dealing with a medical issue. She had a speeding ticket and some other violations, and her car had been booted. For some reason, the court had not received the paperwork on the car being booted, and so we could not address that.

Without her car, how was she going to get Kevante to school? I felt she was a person who needed a break.

I set the cost of removing the boot at $250, allowing both the city and the boot company to collect their fees. Yet this mother was deserving of further consideration.

"Luckily, this country has many generous people," I told Donna. Donor Christian Meshiati had sent a check payable to the Providence Municipal Court, so I was going to use $250 of what he had sent for her.

In tears, Donna said, "Thank you so much, and thank you, Mr. Meshiati." I only asked her to take care of her son, who I am convinced will one day do remarkable things. I often tell children that I am expecting them to leave my courtroom and go on to do great things. The power in knowing someone expects greatness from you is immeasurable. I am certain that people feel inspired to do their best because along the way someone told them they believed in them. I am certain that I became an attorney, and in time a judge, because my father and mother told me I could be one.

Imagine if all of us did more acts of generosity, and we told more people that we believed in them—how much better we could make the world!

I let Donna know, "I hope you remember to pay Mr. Meshiati's kindness forward to someone else who is in need." And, in turn, I hope they do the same for someone else. Every act of compassion, no matter how small, has the potential to go on forever touching lives.

Remember, if we really want more kindness in the world, it's up to us to put it out there.

CHAPTER 21

The Importance of Being a Good Neighbor and a Good Friend

Sometimes all you need to do to help someone is to be there for them. I saw that often in my courtroom, as was the case with Harriet Singer and Frances Gordon.

Harriet was an elderly woman who turned up in my court with a speeding ticket. She fully admitted that she was speeding in a school zone. She explained that she had brought gazpacho to a friend who was just home from the hospital, and was herself returning home. She had no real excuse.

However, in conversation with Harriet, I learned several important facts: she was ninety-one and had never had a ticket before, after more than seventy years of having a license! She was driving in the school zone on a day when school was closed. And she was in court that day with a neighbor, Frances, who drove her there because Harriet was nervous about appearing in court.

I was touched by the fact that Harriet had a neighbor who cared enough to bring her to court, and that reflected well on both of them. Harriet and Frances understood the benefits of being good neighbors, and I encourage everyone to take a page out of their book. Life is so much richer when you know your neighbors. Plus, you never know when you are going to need to borrow a cup of sugar—or in our case, on Federal Hill, a can of Italian tomatoes.

I teased Harriet that at ninety-one, she was going wild with all the speeding and partying. We all laughed about that. Then I told Harriet that since this was her first traffic offense, I was going to dismiss her ticket, as long as I didn't see her again in court for another ninety-one years!

On another occasion, another older woman came to my courtroom with a parking violation ticket. She explained that she was bringing food to a sick friend.

I decided to dismiss the ticket because I did not feel she should be punished for doing a good deed. Hearing about her bringing food to a sick friend brought back fond memories of my mother doing the same thing.

On Federal Hill, we lived in a tight-knit community. The benefits were endless. As neighbors, we supported each other emotionally, physically, and, when needed, financially. We played together, we ate together, we celebrated together, and we grieved together. We were stronger together, and we were happier together. The key is: we were all in it together.

Bringing food to a sick friend or neighbor is a beautiful and helpful tradition. Sadly, it's rarely practiced anymore.

Let's change that. If you have a sick friend, one who's recently had a baby, or someone who's lost a loved one, show them how much you care for them and cherish their friendship by cooking them something special. Trust me, you will not only be feeding a friend, but you will also be nourishing your own soul. I cannot emphasize enough that it is vital to our own well-being to help others out. So often it does so much more for the one giving than the one receiving.

CHAPTER 22

You Never Stop Being a Parent

One of the most popular of all the cases we have ever shown, and a personal favorite of mine, involved Victor Colella, who was charged with exceeding the speed limit in a school zone.

Victor, who was white-haired and walked with the aid of a cane, sat down, and told me, "I don't drive that fast, Judge. I'm ninety-six years old, and I drive slowly, and I only drive when I have to." Then he said, by way of explanation, "I was going to the blood work for my boy. He's handicapped."

To clarify, I asked, "You're taking your son to the doctor's office?"

"Yes, I take him for blood work," he answered, "every two weeks because he's got cancer."

"You're a good man," I said. "Here you are in your nineties, and you're still taking care of your family. That's just wonderful."

He told me his son was sixty-three.

"Daddy's still taking care of him," I said, and then pointed to my own son David, who was sitting in the courtroom. I teased Victor that he was setting a bad example, and that because of him, when I was in my nineties, I would still be driving David around. I was kidding, of course.

What I said to Victor was: "I wish you all the best. I wish the best for your son. And I wish you good health. And," I added, "your case is dismissed."

⚖

I don't usually see defendants again, but in this case, that was not the end of our encounter. Several months later, David and I went to Mr. Colella's home to hear him tell us his life story.

Born in 1923, he grew up on Federal Hill with six sisters. "I couldn't get a word in edgewise," he said. "They were always telling me what to do."

He told us that he ended up marrying his next-door neighbor, and they had one girl, Laura, and a boy, Richard. Bringing up his family, he said, was his "greatest accomplishment."

When I asked him what advice he would give to people coming up today, he said, "Young kids, please don't smoke, don't drink, be honest, go to church every Sunday." He added, "Don't bully anybody . . . [Bullies] take advantage of the weak people. Try to help the people who are weaker than you. God was put on this earth to help everybody. So, I look at it this way: if he can help everybody, I can help anybody else, too."

With Victor Colella

Three years later, when Victor was ninety-nine, David and I went to visit him at his home again, to get an update on his life and his son's health. His son, Richard, was cancer free, and Victor served us a slice of homemade apple pie—which was the best apple pie I ever had!

David and I then invited him to our home to teach us how to make one of his pies. It was a delicious cooking lesson that we filmed and posted on social media.

When Victor turned one hundred, David and I surprised him with a cake at his home. He started to cry when we walked in the door. It was a touching moment for all of us, all because Victor got a ticket while being a good father to his son.

We also went to the Johnston Senior Center, in Johnston, Rhode Island, to join in the celebration of Victor's one hundredth birthday, at which Johnston's mayor, Joseph Polisena Jr., presented him with a special proclamation in his honor from the city.

Victor Colella, through his appearance on *Caught in Providence*, has touched and inspired millions of people, yet his story is also a shining example of how a long life well lived is its own greatest reward.

CHAPTER 23

The World Isn't Against You

When a person is angry, stubborn, or difficult, it is hard to have empathy or compassion for them. Generally, when someone appeared in my courtroom, and they were rude to an officer or clerk of the court, I had little sympathy for them.

Over the years, however, I learned that the attitude that others brought with them was not always where the conversation should start. I often began by asking them to tell me what was going on in their life.

Sometimes life can be downright overwhelming, and with those stressful situations, anger and frustration can lead someone to lash out at innocent people, like friends or family—or in Pam's situation, the clerks in our traffic division.

Pam came to court because her car had been booted. She began by telling me that she had come to court earlier and paid $95 but then got into such a fight with the clerks there that she almost got arrested.

That was not the whole story, as I told Pam. She had fifteen unpaid tickets and four red light violations, and her car had been booted more than once. Pam had her own reasons as to why she didn't obey the traffic laws and believed that she shouldn't have been ticketed each time. She was unwilling to take any responsibility and admit any guilt.

As I tried to get Pam to listen to me, her eyes began to well up with tears. I could tell there was more to her story. I asked Pam what was going on in her life.

"Everything," she said. Pam explained that her son had autism and ADHD and obedience issues, and he had to attend school in the summer. She needed to personally help her son on and off the school bus, but there was no parking available on her street and no lot nearby.

She explained that when she came to court a month before, she had just paid $695 to get the boot lifted from her car and was there to pay the two tickets she owed. However, she was told there were another four that she had not paid. It was overwhelming. She further explained that she had five children: an eighteen-year-old, a twelve-year-old, eleven-year-old twins, and a five-year-old.

Although I rarely had compassion for people who came into my court with a bad attitude or who were rude to the clerks, it was obvious that Pam was acting out of frustration. When she spoke with city officials who saw the facts of her tickets and fines differently than her, or were not sympathetic to her reasons, she became even more frustrated and acted harshly toward them. It made me think of how I behaved toward the woman who appeared before me on my first day as a judge. I wasn't going to take that approach again.

I told Pam that I understood that she was filled with frustration, that she had five kids, and that money was tight.

"Take a deep breath and understand the world isn't against you," I said. "Everybody isn't trying to get you." I tried to have Pam understand that most of her problems were of her own making. Right now, her circumstances had power over her. Pam needed to get better control of her circumstances, whether it was getting a park pass or a handicapped placard, and obey the traffic laws.

I gave Pam a break on the fine for her car being booted and arranged a payment plan for the tickets that she could live with. I hoped that she would come to see that the world wasn't against her, and that having a good attitude would serve her cause better than arguing with those who were just doing their jobs and following the law.

CHAPTER 24

A Nation of Immigrants

I grew up very conscious of the hard work of immigrants, many of whom literally built our nation. This remains true for each successive wave of immigrants.

Every day as a judge for the Providence Municipal Court, I saw a parade of immigrants come before me; it is through them that I'm reminded that unity is our strength and diversity is our power.

Chief Inspector Robert "Ziggy" Quinn, whom you may know from my videos (he has since retired), is a cop's cop. He is well respected. He earned his stripes on the streets of Providence and rose through the ranks to become head of prosecutions for the City of Providence. He is as proud of his Irish heritage as I am of my Italian one. We were always sensitive to slights immigrants faced when they appeared in court.

One time, Carlos Peixinho came before me in court and asked me to repeat his last name correctly, which I did. Inspector Quinn identified his name as Portuguese, but I corrected him. "That's American," I said, "with a proud Portuguese heritage."

Carlos was seven years old when he came to the United States. He became an American citizen. That makes him just as American as any other citizen of this proud nation.

To Carlos, I pointed out that Inspector Quinn's ancestors were from Ireland; my family was from Italy. "With the exception of Native Americans, everyone here," I said, "has someone at some point in their life that came from a different country. So, we are all brothers and sisters."

On another occasion, Francisco Haridia de los Santos appeared before me. He had come to the United States from the Dominican Republic. He was married with three children, two boys and a girl. He worked for a social service organization driving senior citizens to their doctor's appointments. He had multiple tickets, he explained, due to the closing of a bridge in his neighborhood that two years later was still under repair, causing all sorts of traffic problems that were the reason for the violations he received.

His English was not good, but it was clear he loved his family and helping others. He was a good citizen and a hardworking person. I decided to reduce his fines, and to pay for them I used some of the funds in the court's discretionary account, the Filomena Fund, which consisted of donations from people all over the country and all over the world.

When I told Mr. de los Santos that he would not have to pay for his fines, I asked how he felt. He answered in Spanish: *agradecido*, which means grateful.

"This is a great country, a great people, a great system [of justice]," he said, noting that it was much different than in the Dominican Republic. "Here you have freedom . . . And freedom is life."

That was heartwarming for me to hear. Immigrants often value what we take for granted.

★

George Washington once wrote, "I had always hoped that this land might become a safe and agreeable asylum to the virtuous and persecuted part of mankind, to whatever nation they might belong."

I agree with our founding father, and I want our country to remain a shining beacon to people all over the world.

Let me share one of the most amazing stories that occurred because of my courtroom videos, one that gives me hope. One day I got a message from Ahmed Ahmad, a social researcher in Iraq. He wrote, "I am from Iraq where wars, explosions, and the sound of bullets are part of my daily life. I am now fifty years old, and since I was born my country has not lived a single day of peace." He had translated one of our court cases into Arabic and posted it on his Facebook page. And within days more than a million Iraqis had watched the video. He wrote, "All of those who watched this video wept at the sound of peace in the tone of your voice which they have not felt for decades."

I want to thank Ahmed for his powerful personal message. It reminded me just how fortunate I am that my grandfather decided to risk it all and come to America to seek a better life for his family.

I have tremendous compassion for all those living under harsh conditions in foreign lands and have empathy for those who come to the United States in search of a better life.

America is a land of immigrants. Our ancestors were drawn to this country because our founders had the inspirational belief that we are all created equal, endowed by our creator with the right to life, liberty, and the pursuit of happiness.

Today, living up to that profound moral foundation continues to be a test of our nation's character.

CHAPTER 25

The Strength of Women

If someone were to tell me that women have a greater capacity for compassion and empathy than men, I would not argue with them. My grandmother and mother set the standard for me.

The strength of women never fails to humble me. They are uniquely equipped with the emotional, spiritual, and psychological strength to shoulder the everyday burdens of life.

Jacqueline Rodrigues was an example of the strong women who came into to my courtroom. Just three days before, while walking by a park, she had been shot in the leg. When she appeared in court, the bullet was still in her leg. The surgeons had determined that removing it would cause greater damage.

Jacqueline explained that she worked at the convention center from 6 PM to midnight and had left about half an hour early to catch the bus home. She was walking by a park near the bus stop when she heard a bunch of shots go off. Instinctively, she began to run and discovered that she was limping because she had been hit. She was a random innocent victim of gun violence. "I was at the wrong place at the wrong time," she said.

She was in court regarding a ticket that she got for parking in front of her own house, while running in to help one of her children who was breathing from an oxygen tank. The car was in her father-in-law's name, so she showed up because she needed to take responsibility.

I was so impressed with this young woman, a mother of four, who showed up in court regarding a ticket with a bullet still in her leg. She later told me that she worked two jobs a day so she could pay for her son's oxygen canisters.

Jacqueline was an angel among us, an example of good attitude and selfless behavior we should all emulate. I dismissed her ticket.

Another angel I would like to single out is Freida Adams-Hughes. My courtroom has seen several impressive foster parents over the years, but none like Freida. She came before me more than once. She was a very down-to-earth person who came to court for the first time to admit her guilt regarding a parking ticket. She had to take responsibility and admit her wrong, she said, because she knew God was watching her and wanted her to speak the truth.

She had, over many, many years, fostered twenty-seven children. She did so, she said, "to put them on the right path, and keep them from the negative."

When she appeared in court the second time, she shared that she had adopted one of the children she fostered, and she had just sent him off to college with a scholarship he earned. "I did a good job with him," she said. "I had him since he was eleven. I saw great potential in that child. I knew he was going somewhere in life. All he needed was a hand to lift him and to direct him on the right path."

Freida told the court that "God wants us to help the less fortunate."

I couldn't agree more. But in Freida's case, it was clear that she was the one her kids modeled their behavior on and that they learned so much from how she conducted herself and the example she set for them. She had taught them not how to make a living, but how to live life.

⚖

On one occasion, Gabriella V. came to court with her daughter. Gabriella was wearing a headscarf, which could well have been a fashion statement or a religious choice. But there was another reason: she had been having radiation treatments for breast cancer.

Her daughter explained that her mother had gotten a ticket for running a red light rushing to her last day of treatment. Her situation reminded me of a saying of which I'm particularly fond: "See the world through the eyes of the people you are speaking to."

Gabriella unquestionably ran that red light. And it was clear that she was in a rush. But when I saw the event through her eyes, with what she was going through, she was clearly a good mom going through a tough time and keeping a positive attitude. To me, that was worth a lot. I dismissed her ticket.

⚖

On another memorable occasion, Michelle Verdejo, a single parent, came to court with Arion, her twelve-year-old son. When I asked him to speak, Arion informed us that he had autism and ADHD. He was incredibly well-spoken, thoughtful, and mature for his age.

I have seen many parents of special needs children in my courtroom. They are great examples of the adage "True parenthood is about raising the child you have, not the child you thought you would have." Raising any child is challenging, but parenting a child with special needs will teach you just how strong you really are. It requires incredible tenacity, patience, resourcefulness, and an unwavering commitment to never-ending love.

Over the course of her time in court, Michelle spoke about the difficulty of getting a diagnosis for Arion and getting him into the right school. "It took a lot of work," she said. But the results were evident.

"Just because you're different," Arion said, "I don't think you should be treated different, because we are all human beings." That had everyone in the courtroom tearing up, including his mom and me.

Arion also enlightened us to his unique outlook about living with autism. "In a way, I'm proud to have autism," he said, "because it makes me the person that I am."

Michelle had four violations for running red lights. We reviewed them and at least three out of the four were arguably not violations. I brought Arion up to the bench, handed him my gavel, and asked him how we should decide his mother's case.

"Case dismissed," he proclaimed, banging the gavel.

I had to agree.

CHAPTER 26

Cancer Is a Word, Not a Sentence

I am not a doctor, but over my thirty-eight years on the bench, I saw a lot of cancer patients and cancer survivors. Their resilience always impressed me. Just showing up in court was often a challenge. Their strength and courage are the living proof that cancer is a word, not a sentence.

The people I saw in court with cancer are fighters, and even though their cancer may have started the fight, they're the ones who go on to finish it.

I pray and root for them all.

Let me tell one story that moved me beyond measure. A gentleman named Albert Dimaio, or Alberto, as his father-in-law used to call him, appeared in my court. He was white-haired, slightly stooped but solidly built. He was in court concerning a parking ticket. I asked him if he recalled the circumstances under which the ticket was issued.

Albert told me that he was ninety years old and a cancer survivor, but that his hemoglobin gets low. He was at home when he felt so weak that he knew he had to go the hospital. He drove there and parked in the handicapped zone with his handicapped parking placard on display.

At the hospital he was treated by infusion. He was very tired when he left the hospital several hours later, only to discover that his car had been towed away. The tow company charged him $100 to get his car back, and the city gave him a $100 ticket.

It was wrong. I dismissed the ticket.

I hope it meant something to Albert that he had his day in court where he could explain his circumstances and hear a judge agree with him that his ticket was issued erroneously. Just a small measure of kindness and compassion in exchange for the extreme inconvenience he experienced.

On another occasion, Marilyn Ortiz Castillo came before me with three red light violations. She came to court wearing a burgundy turtleneck sweater and a stylish beret that covered her hair.

In her accented English, Marilyn told me that she understood she had responsibility for all her tickets. She explained that one ticket was on her husband's car, and that she received it when she took her asthmatic baby to the hospital because he was having a crisis. She told me that her other tickets occurred while she was being treated for lymphoma. She had been through seven months of chemo and had surgery to remove the cancer. However, the lymphoma had come back. This made her nervous because she had two kids to care for. She understood that she ran the red lights, but she wanted me to know that she was very nervous at the time.

She had not been able to work since she was diagnosed with cancer two years ago because she often did not feel well. She added that her own family and support network were all in the Dominican Republic where she was from; here she only had her husband and his family, and her husband was working.

I asked how she was feeling. "So-so," she answered. She admitted that she was feeling tired, and she always felt cold—her hands were cold all the time.

I asked her to come up to the bench, and I felt her hands, which were very cold.

I told Marilyn that we would be praying for her and hoping that everything went well for her. I wanted her to know that although she had cold hands, there were an awful lot of people in this country who have warm hearts and who reach out to help other people. I told her that occasionally those people sent their donations to the court for me to use as I see fit. I told Marilyn that I was going to use $100 from those funds to pay for her offenses. She would not have to pay anything, as the funds were from people who had great sympathy and compassion.

"I hope that their warm heart can warm your cold hands and also that it can help in your recovery," I told her.

A smile broke out on her face.

While not everyone is able to financially help someone in need, I would like to encourage all of you to find your own way to help the less fortunate. As St. Francis of Assisi said, "For it is in giving that we receive."

CHAPTER 27

Good Health Care Is Critical

In my courtroom, I saw many people with health issues and many parents with children with serious illnesses. All of them struggled with the cost of health care, which troubles me.

According to the United States Census Bureau, in 2022 only 54.5 percent of Americans had health insurance from their employers. Even those who have insurance have seen their premiums and deductibles skyrocket. Unpaid medical bills are now the leading cause of bankruptcy in the United States. It is heartbreaking.

The wealthiest nation in the history of the world should be able to come up with a path for everyone to have access to top-quality health care. I don't pretend to know the solution. However, if we all pull together—health care providers, physicians and health care workers, insurers, and average citizens—perhaps we can shoulder this burden together with each side giving a little more so we can all lead healthier lives.

It has always been my policy to dismiss tickets received when someone was getting themselves or their loved ones the good health they so deserve.

For example, a young woman appeared in court before me one day. Her head was bandaged, with wires leading to a device that I assumed was part of her treatment. She explained that she was being treated for seizures.

She had received a $75 ticket and had paid $55 with a note that she would pay the balance of $20 in a few weeks after she had paid for her medications. But she had received notice that the city was now fining her $225 for that same ticket. She had come to court to ask if she could pay the balance of $20 that she had promised to pay instead of the $225 she was being charged.

I could remember when $20 to me was a matter of survival, which is why I understood that $20 was a lot of money to a young woman who had serious medical issues and had already paid $55.

I dismissed all her fines.

Another time, a young woman came into my courtroom to challenge a $30 parking ticket. I had a feeling that she had a reason why she was willing to fight this ticket. But I was surprised by what she told me. She had a broken heart. But not in the way that you think.

She said that she had started a new job at Brown University a few months prior. On her second day on the job, she collapsed. It turned out that she had a SCAD—a spontaneous coronary artery dissection, which means that a piece of her heart valve broke off, causing a heart attack. There was no real cause for SCAD and, in her case, no real explanation for it happening. Nonetheless, she was grateful to have survived.

Several months after her heart attack, the woman was to return to work, part-time at first. She spent forty minutes looking for a parking spot, and when a car gave one up, she took it. She saw no signs posted that it was not a legal parking spot.

I asked her if her medical crisis had changed her outlook on life. She said that knowing you can die at any moment is hard to adjust to, but she had always had a positive outlook.

I told her that we were all rooting for her. I also mentioned that having a near-death experience makes many more appreciative of life.

"Enjoy every day of life because life is a precious gift," I told her. We dismissed the case.

Good health care for all is so important because we never know when we might have a health crisis. When someone we know is ill, we would all move heaven and earth to see them get the proper treatment. The United States has been a refuge and a lifeline for so many; we must find a way for our country to offer people health care they can afford.

Too often, we are made to believe that someone else's health care, particularly those who can't afford it, comes at our own expense. But the cost of sickness, and the impact of children living with sick parents or without parents because they died due to poor health care, is so much greater. Let us act out of compassion: together we can afford what each one of us individually can't.

CHAPTER 28

Human Tragedies

We all know life isn't fair. Sometimes, people who appeared in my courtroom had experienced such terrible tragedies and were suffering on so many fronts that I could not add to their burden. One case I can't forget is that of Andrea Rogers.

Andrea appeared before me with eleven tickets on two different cars: a set of five tickets that went back a decade, two more a few years later, and four recent parking tickets.

I told Andrea we would not be pursuing the decade-old tickets, just the six more recent ones.

Andrea then teared up as she explained that she received the first of those tickets when she had gone to the Social Security office, which had stopped her payments because her son had been overpaid $75 and that money needed to be returned. Her son, however, was deceased. He'd been murdered. But Social Security still demanded repayment and was holding up her payments.

For the second ticket, she related that she had gone to court because her landlord was evicting her. While she was in court, the parking meter had run out of time, and she'd received a ticket. Meanwhile, the landlord had won the case, and she was evicted from her home.

Another time, she went to legal services to get help, and while she was getting change at Dunkin' Donuts for the parking meter, she got a $100 parking ticket.

"It's like I can't win," Andrea said. "I've had a tough year." She said she was still paying for her son's funeral. "I don't know where this money is supposed to come from."

And then she shared the most heartbreaking part of her story: her brother was the one who killed her son. She blamed herself for not being able to deescalate the situation.

Andrea had experienced terrible trauma. I was not going to add to her burden, financial or otherwise, so I dismissed the fines for her parking tickets.

Sometimes it really does seem, as Andrea put it, that you can't win. But just because it is raining doesn't mean the sun will never shine again. There is a bumper sticker I once saw that expresses what may seem trite but is true: "No rain, no rainbow."

"This too shall pass" is another popular refrain, but it really is true.

It's hard to believe how much you come to know about a person's story by hearing what they have to say in traffic court. All it took was for me to gently ask her what was going on and let her know she could trust baring her soul. I was not going to embarrass her; I was not going to act awkwardly when she talked about her suffering. In short, I created a safe environment so she could open up and be vulnerable. While her suffering is clearly immense, I hope her knowing I cared about what she had to share and that I understood she was going through a very rough period offered some small measure of comfort. It was my hope that Andrea would hang in there, stay the course, and find her way to better times.

Andrea's traffic case was aired on television and social media. A follower on our Facebook page started a GoFundMe account to help Andrea. We had no involvement at all. The viewers responded by donating more than $50,000.

Several months later, my son David saw Andrea in the family court helping a friend. She told him that she paid her outstanding bills and was using the rest of the money to buy a house so that her family would never have to worry again about being evicted. Andrea was still suffering from her losses, but knowing that hundreds of total strangers gave her a lifeline filled her with hope and gratitude.

CHAPTER 29

Dealing with Grief

Death and loss come into all our lives. Being the nephew in a family of eighteen aunts and uncles means that I have attended a lot of funerals.

My older brother, Anthony, was a great person. As I mentioned earlier, he was my protector. We worked on the milk truck together; we shared a room for many years. He was my inspiration. In his younger days, he was a great athlete and played football, so I played football. He served in the military and afterward became a police officer and then a teacher, eventually rising to be the principal of Hope High School and Mount Pleasant High School in Providence. So I knew I could be a teacher, too. He died a few years ago, and not a day goes by that I don't think of him and miss him terribly. My memories of him inform my actions every day.

Shortly after I lost Anthony, a man called John Rose appeared in court before me. When I asked him how he was doing, it was clear

With my brothers, Anthony (*left*) and Joe (*right*), and our father, Tup

he wasn't doing very well. But first, he passed along his condolences on the loss of my brother Anthony.

John told me that he had met Anthony at a local breakfast spot. When John and his wife went there one day, it was crowded and there were no seats available, and it seemed like others who had arrived after them were being seated before them.

Whether that was because the couple was Black is not certain. But Anthony did something Tup would have done: he was sitting at a table by himself, and he invited John and his wife to join him at his table. They quickly discovered Anthony was quite the character. Anthony picked up the breakfast tab that day.

That was Anthony.

For many years after that, John and his wife met weekly to have breakfast with Anthony at that same diner. It's one of countless examples of how my older brother touched people. He learned from my mother and father to approach life with an open heart and in return he was always surrounded by the most wonderful people.

"Anthony had the biggest heart in the world," said John.

Then John explained why he was in court: he'd gone through a red light because his dogs were with him in the car, they had seen another dog, were excited, and distracted him. But he fully admitted that he ran the red light.

I asked to see the video. Yes, his car did run the red light, but the timer noted "0.3"—meaning he had only been three tenths of a second late.

I dismissed his ticket, explaining that I wasn't giving him a break because he knew my brother. This was what I would do for anyone who had only been three tenths of a second late.

John thanked me and told me he thought of Anthony often, particularly when he and his wife went for breakfast.

I think of Anthony every day and mourn his loss. I have great compassion for those who are suffering from grief. Grief is a complex emotion that can overwhelm people. I can't say it ever gets better, but over time you grow to live with it.

Grief can also be overpowering. One morning, a young man named Mario Farw appeared in my courtroom because of a school-zone violation and a red-light violation. Mario said although he was not sure if he came to a pause at the red light or not, he was in court not to argue but to take responsibility for what he did. What Mario wanted was to get on a payment plan. He explained that he was having financial difficulty because his father had passed away and left him a lot of debt. "I'm a man," he said. "I messed up. I pay for my mistakes."

When I asked him when his father had passed, he immediately teared up and said it was just a few months ago. I said it was clear they were close. "It's not that we were close," Mario explained, but rather that they had been trying to rebuild their relationship. His mother and father had divorced when he was a child, and he and his father had not been close after that. "We had gotten over the hump, and then he was just ripped out of my life," he said, breaking down.

Mario then revealed that he had got one of his tickets while going to visit his 100-year-old grandmother who claimed she was a neighbor of mine.

When he told me her name, of course I knew her. Many years ago, we lived in a tenement house that had eight apartments. We lived on the second floor, and Mario's grandmother lived on the first floor.

I told Mario that a kind woman named Connie Maytok had sent in $50 to help others, which I would use to pay the fines he owed. He was grateful.

There can be great loneliness associated with grief. Many of us don't know what to say to someone who has lost a loved one. We worry that we'll say the wrong thing, so we say nothing at all. Or we tell ourselves that people need space when what we're really doing is avoiding our own uncomfortable feelings. The best thing you can do for someone who is grieving is to show up for them. Let them know you care and love them.

Often, we wonder: *What can we do?* The answer is simple: have compassion.

If you know someone who is grieving, please reach out to them. It is okay not to have all the right words. As an old Swedish proverb says so well, "A true friend doubles our joy and divides our grief."

CHAPTER 30

A Helping Hand to Others

Mahatma Gandhi once said that "the true measure of any society can be found in how it treats its most vulnerable members."

The United States has one of the largest prison populations in the world. Each year, according to the National Institute of Corrections, the United States spends $80 billion on public prisons. It often costs more to keep someone in jail for a year than it does to send them to college. However, the true cost of their confinement runs much deeper: two out of three families of the incarcerated cannot afford basic necessities. The problems that are left behind by those who are incarcerated should not fall on their families or significant others. Nonetheless, I have often seen the impact of these problems in my courtroom.

One morning, an elementary school teacher named Jenna Bettez came into my courtroom. She was standing before me on a summer morning when school was not in session. In her arms was her young son, Luke, and there was a baby, Bella, in a sling around her neck. Two tickets had been issued to a car registered in her name.

Jenna explained that the tickets for which she was appearing in court were all received by the father of her children. He was not present because he was in jail. She had shown up in court because the tickets were filed on a car she owned, and even though she was not the cause of the tickets, she was prepared to take responsibility for them.

The letter of the law would have had me collect fines for those tickets. The car was registered in her name, and that was that. But I knew those tickets were not her doing and paying them would cause her greater financial and personal hardship. Seeing that the tickets were not her fault, and that she was not only a good mother but also a teacher who would have an important impact on the lives of many children, I dismissed the charges and fines against her. That money needed to be spent on Luke and Bella.

I will always be rooting for the moms out there.

We also need to root for those former convicts who have done their time, seen the errors of their ways, and wanted better lives for themselves and their families. When someone is released from prison, having served their time, it is in our society's best interest for those people to find a good job and a place to live.

One morning, a young man named Kyle Mellow appeared in court with his six-year-old son, Caden. He had received a ticket for not yielding in a crosswalk, not wearing a seat belt, and not having a license.

Kyle explained that he had spent almost three years in jail. During that time, his license had expired, and he was working to get it back, but he needed to take courses that cost $800. He explained that when he was ticketed, he was driving his son to his mother, who was living in Newport, Rhode Island. He knew he shouldn't have been driving, but he had no other way to get Caden to his mother's.

Punishing Kyle for trying to be a responsible parent and delaying his getting his license was not going to help anyone—and it was certainly going to hurt his family. I ended up dismissing some of the violations and using the discretionary fund of donations to the court to pay his fines.

I asked Kyle what he was doing to straighten himself out.

He answered that he was working as a cook at a tavern in East Providence. "I cook and my days off I'm with him," he said, referring to Caden. "That's all I do. I'm trying to stay out of trouble. And get in my classes, which are on Saturdays. Just trying to get everything done."

I told him, "It's not a crime to get knocked down, but it's a sin not to get back up. Think of your son. You've been in prison, and you don't want to go back. Put it behind you. There are good people who want to help you. But you have to help yourself." Kyle said he understood. I hope he took my advice to heart.

Unfortunately, it takes some people several trips to prison before they can change their ways.

When Jeffrey Turner appeared in my courtroom, he was only thirty-six years old, but he had spent almost half of his life in prison. He was then living in an apartment with his girlfriend and their child. He had come to court to resolve tickets that were preventing him from having a license and being able to drive, which made it difficult to hold a steady job.

He presented himself with such great sincerity and humility that I was inclined to give him a second chance. I decided to place my faith in Jeffrey, believing that he saw life on the outside as better than returning to prison. I dismissed his tickets and the charges he had incurred, which cleared the way for him to get his driver's license reinstated.

Too often, tickets and fines mount while people are in jail. When they get out, they are saddled with fines they cannot pay. Often their licenses have been suspended because of their unpaid tickets, making it next to impossible for them to seek employment and get their lives back on track. We need to remove these hurdles as much as possible for the good of us all. We all win when someone returning to society can contribute meaningfully.

The Bible commands us: "Before a blind man, do not place a stumbling block." There need to be more bridges built to help those getting their lives back on track.

On another occasion, I had a young man named Rodney Goudein in my courtroom. He wanted to turn his life around, but because he had been in prison, he was finding it difficult to find anyone who would hire him.

Rodney's not alone. Nearly one third of working-age Americans have criminal records. Yet only one out of eight employers will consider hiring them. That leaves many qualified and willing workers on the sidelines. According to an article by Timothy McNutt, the director of Criminal Justice and Employment Initiative of Cornell University's School of Industry and Labor Relations (ILR), human resources managers found that annual turnover was on average 12.2 percent lower for employees with criminal records, and adopting a program to recruit employees with criminal histories reduced turnover from 25 percent to 11 percent.

I would like to encourage all employers to consider hiring those who've done their time. It just makes sense with so many businesses struggling to find workers: Why not give them a chance? You will have the opportunity to transform lives, reunite families, and rebuild communities. There are several fine organizations that are dedicated to helping businesses connect with the formerly incarcerated such as the Prison Entrepreneurship Program (www.pep.org), as well as similar organizations devoted to reducing recidivism.

If you can make that happen for someone who is looking to turn their life around, please do so. You will be rewarded for your trust and kindness.

CHAPTER 31

Being a Criminal Is Addictive

s important as it is to regard others with compassion, we need to be clear that even compassion has its limits.

No matter how much we would like to believe in the better angels of people's natures, the truth is that many criminals return to crime. One exemplary case that came before me stands out, and it stands out for others, too. This video has been watched by more than 50 million viewers. It is the case of one of the most unforgettable characters to turn up in my court, William Sequeira.

When he first appeared in my courtroom, William was in his mid-fifties. He was driving a truck delivering produce. He had received three traffic tickets; he wasn't sure how or why. Then he told me that he had spent thirty-seven years of his life in jail—thirty in federal prison and seven in state penitentiaries.

William had been a bank robber. He told me that in his career he had robbed maybe 150 banks and armored trucks. Sometimes he robbed the same bank twice. The most he had taken in a single bank robbery, he estimated, was $500,000. He used to keep $400,000 hidden in his refrigerator. He claimed that he was the inspiration for Ben Affleck's character Doug MacRay in *The Town* (2010).

William told me that his father's death when he was eight years old caused him to act out, landing him in the foster care system. When he was eighteen, he moved to Boston, where he started hanging out at the Triple O's Lounge, the bar where Whitey Bulger, who led the Irish mob in Boston, held court. In no time, Sequeira became part of a robbery crew. The adrenaline of committing a robbery, he said, was addictive. He carried a stopwatch, and they committed the robberies in under sixty seconds.

"It was: Get in, grab, and get out," he said. "I had a lot of money."

But he also ended up getting caught, in what he said was one of the largest police chases in Rhode Island history, landing him in federal prison.

"No one wants to go to federal penitentiary," he explained. "It's a very bad world in there. Very violent, real serious." He went on to tell me that federal prison was a place of danger, of assaults where he was stabbed and had to stab others, and where the only way to stay safe was to be part of a gang. In every federal prison in New England there were Boston criminals, which was the gang he joined. He showed a "B" tattooed by his ear that indicated his gang membership.

However, one day while he was in federal prison in Atlanta, he received a letter under his cell door. It informed him that there was a recent Supreme Court decision, *Johnson v. United States*, that determined that the Armed Career Criminal Act defined "violent felony" in a way that was unconstitutionally vague, and because of it, they had reviewed all the convictions under that act, including his.

"Your case fits the criteria of the Johnson case," the letter described. "You're going to be going back to the Federal [District] Court in Providence and you're going to get an immediate release from prison."

William was again a free man. It was now three years since his release. He'd found a job and said he had no intention of ever returning to prison. Because he seemed to have turned his life around, I decided to give him a break. I only fined him $150 for the three tickets, and to pay for it I used $150 from the Filomena Fund, donated by Chuck Shaheen, the former mayor of Warner Robins, Georgia.

William Sequeira's appearance in my courtroom for his three red-light tickets caused so much interest, my son David and I decided to visit him to hear his story in greater detail. Once again, he said he had given up his life of crime and was never going back to prison.

Unfortunately, after three years of freedom, fifty-nine-year-old William Sequeira, or "Boston Billy" as the press dubbed him, appeared in court in Boston on charges that he had robbed four banks in Boston in four days and was apprehended trying to rob a fifth. He ended up pleading guilty and was sentenced to fifty-four months in prison for his crimes.

This is not a new story. I have seen statistics saying that 77 percent of those released from prison end up being rearrested within five years. And that is despite knowing how awful prison life is.

Sometimes our best efforts, our best intentions, and even the promises of those involved cannot keep a person from a life of crime. That does not mean we should stop helping others. In fact, it is even more reason to support former inmates who want to turn their lives around.

CHAPTER 32

Homeless but Not Helpless

Homelessness is a national epidemic for which we don't yet have the cure. Still, being homeless does not have to be a permanent condition for a person or a family. There are many people working hard to emerge from homelessness, and many organizations and individuals working to help them. I know this because I saw it often in my courtroom. Their compassion was always inspiring.

A case that broke my heart was that of Carl Smith. When Carl appeared before me, he shared that it had been a tough year. He was homeless and living in his car. He had spent forty years as a newspaper delivery man. He had made a $10 payment toward a parking fine and still owed $20.

I canceled the rest of what he owed. I had Inspector Quinn give Carl $50 in cash from the Filomena Fund, hoping he would use it to get a healthy meal and a decent place to sleep.

Sadly, Carl's situation is far from unique, because of the lack of affordable housing. The U.S. Department of Housing and Urban Development (HUD) 2022 Annual Homeless Assessment Report estimated that 582,500 people in the United States were experiencing homelessness on a single night in 2022. Compounding their troubles, many communities have now made it a crime to live in your car. Many nonprofit organizations are trying a more compassionate approach by implementing safe parking programs where the homeless can safely stay overnight in designated parking lots. Many of these lots are staffed with caseworkers who help people like Carl find permanent housing.

I encourage everyone to support your local homeless organizations. Everyone deserves the dignity and safety of a warm bed.

Another case that affected me was that of Tisha Miller. She appeared in court with a lawyer from a legal clinic and with Megan Smith, a social worker from House of Hope, a Providence community aid organization that has been working to end homelessness since 1989 by providing safe, stable housing to their clients.

Her attorney explained that Tisha had experienced homelessness for an extended period during which she was living in and out

of her car, and that she had accumulated the parking tickets cul-
minating in her car being booted because Providence won't issue
a parking permit to someone without a permanent address. With
Megan Smith's help, Tisha had very recently secured housing.

She was in court with her young daughter, Jemiah. I asked how
many children she had. She said she had four altogether, but three
were already grown. She had her youngest daughter when she was
forty-one.

I asked Tisha if she was working. She told me that she suffered
from fibromyalgia, but that House of Hope was helping her get
social security. "I was stuck in a hole, it felt like, for a really long
time," she said. But now there was hope, thanks to House of Hope,
the Rhode Island Coalition to End Homelessness, and people such
as Megan Smith. "They love their job," she said. "These are the best
people I have met in a long, long time. They really have been helping me. And I really do appreciate their help. They just made me
feel like somebody again."

She explained that she had seen Megan and her coworkers
helping others in a parking lot. She approached Megan and asked
if they could help her. "She said yes and since that day they've been
helping me turn my life around."

I told Tisha that I was going to dismiss all the charges and fines
against her. In addition, using money from the Filomena Fund, I
gave her $50 on the spot to take with her.

Tisha was overwhelmed. "Your honor, I don't have a dollar to
my name. I really thank you for that, I really do." With tears in her
eyes, she added, "You don't understand. I woke up this morning
and I said: I need milk, I need this, I need that. But I decided, I'm
not going to worry about that, I'm going to go to court." She was

crying as she continued, "I really appreciate it. So many people have recently done nice things for me. And I never have people do nice things for me . . . I feel blessed."

Her daughter Jemiah then asked me, "Can I give you a hug?" Which she did.

If you have not seen this video, please watch it: it's called "House of Hope" and can be found on the *Caught in Providence* social media pages. It is powerful.

You may think the point of this story is how Tisha felt. It is not. It is about the difference Megan Smith, House of Hope, and Tisha's lawyer could make in her and her daughter's lives.

And it's about how getting that hug made me feel.

Help someone else. It is a good feeling.

CHAPTER 33

Everyday Heroes

Our evening news and online news sources are filled with attention-grabbing headlines about criminals. Less time is devoted to the everyday heroes around us whom we should celebrate.

In thinking about this, I am reminded of a young woman who appeared before me. Her name was Veronica. She had run a red light at the intersection of Eddy and Dudley Streets near Rhode Island Hospital.

Veronica told me that she volunteered as a victim advocate for an organization called Day One that specializes in cases of sexual abuse and domestic violence. "Basically," she said, "we are on call whatever time slot we have and [sometimes] we get called to police stations or hospitals." She explained that the day she got the ticket was one of those days, and the woman on whose behalf she was called to advocate had been at the hospital, she said, since 5 AM. "I was rushing because she had been waiting for me for four hours already."

Veronica further explained that most times, she sat with the victims and told them that it was not their fault and they were not the reason for what was going on in their lives. She tried "to give them the support and the resources that many of them need, including [information about] any support groups or shelters."

I was very moved by Veronica and the important volunteer work she was doing.

"At the end of the day," I told her, "that's how we're going to be judged—by the difference we make in the lives that we touch and the hope we inspire in the hopeless."

We watched the video of her car running the light. There was no question she did so.

I asked Inspector Dan Carignan, who was in court that day, what he thought my verdict should be. Inspector Carignan was a highly respected Providence police officer who was very much a straight shooter, and I relied on him to give me an honest law enforcement assessment.

Inspector Carignan told me, "Your honor, we work very closely with Day One." Veronica, he said, "does a wonderful job at what they do in helping the Providence police and prosecutors with these victims."

Inspector Carignan was not prone to exaggeration. Given the circumstances, the case was dismissed.

What strikes me is that the world is full of everyday heroes. People like Veronica, giving back to the community out of the goodness of her heart. I saw this every day in my courtroom, and it heartens me to know there are thousands, millions, of people who care. People who put action behind their sentiments. I believe it is entirely appropriate to take those factors into consideration in my deliberations, and so did Inspector Carignan.

The world needs more people like Veronica. And if you or someone you know is a victim of sexual abuse or domestic violence, please know that there are organizations like Day One to provide the support and resources you need.

CHAPTER 34

Angels Among Us

The Bible says, "Whoever is generous to the poor lends to the lord, and he will repay him for his deed."

Give what you can. You will be repaid tenfold for your generosity.

It takes very little to make a big difference in the lives of others.

There is a Chinese proverb that goes, "If you want happiness for an hour, take a nap. If you want happiness for a day, go fishing. If you want happiness for a year, inherit a fortune. If you want happiness for a lifetime, help somebody."

I saw evidence of this all the time in my courtroom.

Cheryl Bautista, for example, had one red-light violation, a tow-zone parking violation, as well as a five-year-old ticket.

Cheryl explained that for the last twenty years she had been driving disabled veterans to their medical appointments and that on the morning in question, one of the vets she had been regularly driving began coughing up blood. She rushed him to the hospital.

There was no place to park at the VA hospital, so she ended up parking in the tow zone.

Yes, she was wrong for parking there. Yes, she deserved the ticket. Yes, I could enforce the ticket and make her pay for it. I could even add greater penalties and fines.

But if I did all that, it would be proof that I did not really understand what had happened in Cheryl's case.

Cheryl is one of those angels among us, doing God's work. She is more than a good Samaritan; she is an inspiration to us all. She was in an emergency, trying to save a veteran's life. Should she be punished for that?

Tickets dismissed!

Helping others is something we all can do, in ways large and small.

Because of my videos that appear on all social media platforms, I have received letters from all over the country and all over the world from people who want to help others. I want to thank everyone who has done a kind act toward another because of seeing me in court or on my program. And I truly hope that those who were the recipients of a kindness pay it forward by doing something equally considerate for someone else in need. I may be a dreamer, but I passionately believe that simple acts of kindness among strangers can generate a ripple effect from one person to the next, one community to the next. The result can be a kinder, more considerate, more compassionate society—and how great would that be?

Another way to make a difference in your life and in the lives of others is to become a mentor. Not only a great opportunity to become a positive force in a young person's life, it will also give a deeper purpose to yours. Mentors feel a deep sense of productivity: they are reminded that the skills they have honed over a lifetime have value.

If you are interested in becoming a mentor, I would suggest that you volunteer at a local school or your place of worship. You can also go to mentoring.org to find an opportunity in your area. I promise you it is a decision that you will never regret. There are so many people who need help.

So, no matter how you do it, lead the charge. Do something nice for a stranger today and only ask in return that they do the same.

PART THREE

Respect

Respect is one of those words that gets used a lot but practiced little. There are many, many ways to have respect and show respect. Respect is something that should be offered to others regardless of your station in life or that of the other person. It's a question of treating others humanely.

Respect for others is important, but just as necessary is self-respect. How you behave, how you conduct yourself, doesn't only convey respect to others; sometimes it is a way to ask for respect: "Treat others as you would like to be treated" is the golden rule.

It is said in the Bible that the sins of the father should not be visited on the child. But the reverse is also true: even if the father does not deserve respect, your behavior can bring honor to the family name. So, even when dealing with a person who doesn't deserve your respect, such as an abusive parent, a corrupt politician, or a mean teacher or coach, how you behave reflects well on you. I've often referred to this as "keeping your own side of the street clean."

It is my belief, based on a lifetime of experience, that how you conduct yourself can make even the most unreasonable of people act better. And if they don't, if you are satisfied with how you behaved in the situation, you will experience less disappointment. You will know in your heart that you did your best.

Among friends, colleagues, and family, it is important to show respect. Respecting another is a matter of respecting who they are, including their opinions and their unique perspective and experience, even when you don't agree with them. It is truly seeing them and hearing them.

Respect is where all good things begin.

CHAPTER 35

Don't Let Your Anger Get in the Way

There is a popular notion that the tougher a lawyer is for his client, the better he does for him or her. That when the other side screams at you, you need to scream back, and the louder the better. In my experience, nothing could be further from the truth.

If you know someone is angry with you or with your client, then you need a strategy to defuse that anger in a manner that best serves your client. Even if they do not treat you or your client with the respect you believe they deserve, you should still treat your opponent with respect. Let them know you want to be fair with them, and chances are they will eventually come around and be more accommodating than if you were confrontational.

One of the most life-changing successes of my career happened because we did not fight back. Let me explain.

When I lost the race for attorney general, I was not only out of a job—having resigned my city council seat to run—I was also dead broke. So, I returned to the full-time practice of law, eager to take whatever cases came through the door.

One day a woman named Jo Ann came to my office saying she wanted me to represent her in her divorce. Though I was not a divorce lawyer by training, I agreed to represent her.

I learned that her husband, soon to be ex-husband, Richard Oster, was a prominent and very successful businessman in Providence. They had two beautiful young children. Unfortunately, their relationship had soured, and things had turned bitter, as often happens in divorces.

I did my due diligence and discovered that Richard had a reputation as a good person, a good boss, and a philanthropist. However, I also understood that he was very angry at my client.

So, I told Jo Ann that I had a strategy: I was going to reach out to Richard's lawyer and set up a meeting with them at his lawyer's office. I instructed her that when we went to the meeting, she should not talk, no matter what her husband said to provoke her. "Do not respond," I told her. "No matter what."

We had our first meeting, and Richard, with Jo Ann in the room, was saying all kinds of terrible things about what went wrong in his marriage and about his wife. Jo Ann listened to me and did not say anything in response to his venting.

I intentionally let two weeks pass before I called Richard's lawyer again to ask for another meeting. We arrived at his office, and once again Richard let his anger get the best of him. The atmosphere became more confrontational, and his volume escalated. However, my client followed my guidance and did not say anything.

By the third meeting, he had calmed down. With his feelings thoroughly expressed, Richard finally decided to do the right thing, which was to agree to a reasonable settlement. In the end, I was happy, and my client, Jo Ann, was happy. Richard had lived up to his reputation as a reasonable, decent, and generous human being.

Then something unexpected happened. Shortly after the divorce was finalized, I received a call from Richard, who said, "I want to meet with you."

I told him that it was not my practice to meet alone with a recent opposing client. Richard assured me the meeting wasn't about the divorce. He said, "It's about a business matter that I want to discuss with you." Since a new matter would not present a conflict of interest—and because I was still open to taking any opportunity that came through the door—I agreed to the meeting.

When I showed up, Richard had one question for me: "How did you do it?"

"How did I do what?" I asked.

"How did you get me to be so generous to my ex-wife? I was so angry."

I explained that I had a strategy: I knew that he had a reputation as being a decent human being, and that after a while, after he had gotten everything off his chest and out of his system, he would do right by her.

"That's incredible," Richard said. He then said that he wanted to hire me to work for him. I told him I was not sure I could be an in-house corporate attorney.

"I don't want you to work in-house for my company. I want you to work for me as outside counsel, which means that you will be paid much more based on the value of the transactions and your time, not a fixed salary." That was quite an offer!

I accepted and embarked on a friendship that expanded how I saw the world. As fate would have it, Richard's second wife, Sandi, was a former student of mine and a good friend of my wife, Joyce. We raised our families together, traveled together, shared holidays at each other's homes, and considered ourselves to be one big family. Richard became my closest friend until the day he passed away. Sandi and her children remain as close to us as ever.

Imagine that: you represent a guy's wife in his divorce case, and he ends up being one of your best friends. Nobody could have predicted that. But an important lesson is that listening to someone is often a better tactic than fighting them. Showing respect can be a better strategy than disrespecting someone and escalating the conflict.

CHAPTER 36

Your Attitude Matters

First impressions matter in showing proper respect. So does your attitude.

I particularly loved it when someone came before me with a big smile and a good attitude. And it happened most days. Whether I was presiding in court or looking to hire a person for a job, first impressions and attitude were major factors in whom I wanted to help.

I recall a homeless gentleman who came into my court. He had stopped working to care for his dying father. After his father died, he could no longer afford his rent, so he was living out of his utility truck. He was now ready to start looking for work again. Despite all his challenges, he came to court with a positive attitude, wanting to resolve his tickets and move forward in his life.

I asked him how he managed to maintain such a good attitude in the face of so much hardship.

"You have to have a good attitude today, no matter what your circumstances are," he said. "Having a bad attitude is not going to change things, but I think a good attitude has its ways." He believed that facing a bad situation with a good attitude made you better able to deal with hardship and more likely to be able to work through the problem and put it behind you.

I agree. Even in the worst of situations, one should never give up hope. I often tell someone going through a rough patch in their life that they are "in the dryer"—meaning they are getting bounced all around and it feels horrible in the moment. But I encourage them to get through the cycle and know that it will end, and then it is up to them to start on a new path or a fresh start. Resilience pays and a positive attitude brings positive opportunities. All of us enjoy the company of happy, positive people. A good attitude will help you at home, at work, and even occasionally in the courtroom.

Scientific studies, including a 2020 study in the *Journal of Experimental Psychology*, have shown that smiling and laughing, even if faked, changes your brain chemistry. So, even if you do not feel it, forcing a smile or a positive outlook can change your worldview.

A good attitude is infectious.

A good attitude does not cost anything, and it is available to anyone regardless of age, gender, ethnic background, or any other differentiator.

Just as a good attitude can sometimes cut through the negative, a bad attitude can make a problem much worse. Too often, we are the reasons for our problems, and sometimes a bad attitude can become a self-fulfilling prophecy.

It is frustrating when you are trying to help someone and all they do is resist everything you offer. That is often a sign that they understand neither themselves nor the situation they are in. Many times, young people before me tried to act bigger and tougher than they were, for a variety of reasons: courts could be intimidating, and they might have been scared and didn't want to show it. Sometimes, they wanted to look tough to their friends or cared about what others would say. And sometimes, a person had had so many negative experiences that they assumed the worst would occur and that the world was against them. It isn't, but it's often difficult to get through to people who feel that way.

One time in my courtroom, a man approached the bench. He had received a ticket for speeding through a school zone.

"I didn't see the camera there," was his explanation.

"You didn't see the camera," I said, "but you were speeding."

He had a scowl on his face.

"But I have something else I want to address with you," I said. "I have a note here that says you were terribly disrespectful and offensive to the young lady at the clerk's window."

He shook his head and said, "I don't know."

I continued, "I'm going to say what the note says: the note says that you were very rude. The note says: this person came to the window very upset and told her that the mayor should get this ticket and shove it up his . . . And here you used a word that begins with an 'a.' And that you're not going to pay it. That's what you told the woman at the counter."

"No," he began to say, "because . . ."

I cut him off. "I've got news for you. You're going to pay the fine. And if you don't pay for it, your license is going to be suspended. And if you come back again and you're disrespectful at the window, you will pay the consequence. These young ladies are not here to be abused. It's a sign of a coward to yell at a young woman and use that type of language."

"I don't," he said defiantly.

"You want to come back and have a trial on this?" I said. "No? Then you'll pay the full fine right now. And I'm telling you: don't come back and do that again because I won't be so lenient as to just give you a fine."

Inspector Quinn, who always had great insights into the cases we heard, said, "My father told us, 'If you need to yell, yell up.' Meaning if we had a problem, we were expected to man up and take it up with the boss, not yell at the employees."

Good advice, as usual.

⚖

Once, on the same day, I heard the cases of two separate defendants with two completely different attitudes, and two different outcomes.

In the first case, Arthur Lee Holder appeared before me. Arthur was no stranger to me, having already appeared in my courtroom on a previous occasion when he did not make a good impression.

He was belligerent, disrespectful, and dismissive. He didn't do himself any favors with that attitude.

This time, he appeared on a parking violation. He was wearing a team jersey and dark sunglasses in court. When I asked him about the ticket, he denied even being at that location, saying it was in the worst part of Providence. "It's the ghetto and I don't go that place. I don't know where that ticket comes from."

I reminded him that earlier in the day he had met with the city attorney, and that my notes indicated that he had agreed to pay the original $35 fine (his fine was actually $90 now, as it went up each month it remained unpaid, but the court was willing to settle the matter with him for $35).

Arthur disagreed, saying he should not have to pay for a ticket he never received in a place he never went.

I told him that if he disagreed with the resolution he had agreed to earlier, then I would mark him down for trial where the parking officer would tell the court about issuing the ticket, and he could present his defense and the judge would decide.

Arthur wasn't happy about that. He knew he would lose that case.

At this point, I reminded him that the last time he was in my courtroom, after he left, before the door shut, he made an offensive gesture toward me.

Even though we had it on video, Arthur denied making the gesture. "I'm sixty-two years of age. Why would I do something that stupid, your honor? I would never do that."

I then asked him point-blank, "Are you going to pay the $35 or go to trial?"

He agreed to pay the $35 and left court with a scowl on his face. He would turn up in my courtroom several more times with no better attitude and no better result.

But on that day, Arthur's case was followed by that of James Herring, who was polite, deferential, and modest.

James had the physique of a former athlete. Although his size could be intimidating, he was gentle of manner. When I made light of this, he told me that he had three sons, all of whom were taller than him.

He said he told his sons that although they may be bigger than him, he was still the boss. "They give me respect, and that's all I ask for, because my mother and father gave me respect. They taught me how to do that and that's how I live my life."

James was filmed going through a yellow light that turned red, two tenths of a second late. The City of Providence does not prosecute such violations if you are less than two tenths of a second late, so he was just on the line. As I mentioned, however, I allow three tenths of a second in my courtroom. I was also willing to not come down hard on James since he demonstrated respect for the court, for me, and for himself. Giving respect to earn respect is a good way to live your life and a helpful tool to become a happy, successful, and contributing member of your community.

I dismissed his ticket.

CHAPTER 37

Lying to Me Is Lying to Yourself

A lack of respect for others and a lack of self-respect manifests itself in many ways. One of the most common, in my experience, is when someone lies to you or is lying to themselves.

After hearing thousands of cases, I can tell when someone is lying. Their stories lack sufficient detail, or have way too much detail; their eyes look everywhere but at me; or perhaps they change their stories. These are just some of the tip-offs that tell me someone is lying.

Every time someone begins an explanation with "Honestly," or says, "To be fully honest with you," I get suspicious.

In my almost forty years on the bench, I've had quite a few liars appear before me. Often, they did not realize that I or Inspector Quinn or Inspector Carignan already knew the full extent of their misadventures and records. Occasionally, catching someone in a lie can be entertaining, but as it concerns the court, it is a serious matter.

Whatever goodwill I was inclined to dispense toward a defendant vanished when they insisted on telling me falsehoods. There is little point in sharing examples of defendants because regardless of the particulars, the story was always the same: they thought they could get away by lying and that I would not know, and I would dismiss their violations or get the boots off their vehicles. It rarely worked out that way. Inevitably, I informed them that we knew the truth; that they were guilty. I was willing to arrange a payment plan and always hoped that they would behave responsibly going forward. But that was just my hope.

Many times, people think they are more clever than they are. Or more clever than the person they are trying to fool. Sometimes, because they are older and bigger, they attempt to intimidate others. In the short run, they may succeed, but eventually their behavior only succeeds at self-sabotage. They underestimate the intelligence of those who can easily see through their scheming. The people who pick or prey on those they consider weaker rarely triumph in the long run. Eventually life catches up to them. It might take years, but the universe has a way of settling scores. And many such scores were settled in my courtroom!

The same is true about lying. The only person a liar is fooling is themselves.

One evening a young woman stood before me. She seemed quite sincere. Her car had been towed and she hoped to get it back.

She explained that she had been called to her child's school for a meeting. She had parked near the school and put enough money in the meter for an hour and a half. The meeting took four hours and when she emerged, she had a ticket.

However, she was not being entirely truthful about her situation—to me, or to herself.

Here's what really occurred: she had one car that had amassed eleven parking tickets over time, which she had not paid. As a result, her car was towed and impounded. Each day that it sat in impound it collected more fees.

Her solution was to avoid the problem completely by abandoning that car and buying a new one. She imagined that with a new car all her past violations would disappear. That new car was the one that received a parking ticket during the school meeting and that, ostensibly, was why she came to court.

However, when she went to register her new car, the DMV said she had to clear up all her earlier tickets first.

I asked her when her first car was towed. She told me it was several months ago.

Did she know that each day the car was held she incurred more charges? She did. Why, I asked, had she waited so long?

I was angry. Not at the young woman, but for her. It was five months since the car had been towed. That was approximately 150 days, and the tow company at that time usually charged $30 a day to store the car. That amounted to $4,500. That was money she could have used to pay her fines and buy a new car.

I told her what she was doing made no sense. I also told her that omitting facts that were relevant to the matter at hand was a form of lying. It's hard to help someone without all the facts.

None of this looked good to me.

She had to be more responsible. She could not hide her head in the sand and ignore those things she didn't want to deal with.

I asked her what she could pay. She said she was not working now but would be next month, and she wanted to arrange a payment plan.

What I didn't want to happen was for her to promise she would pay and then not be able to do so.

I knew that it was not going to serve any useful purpose to fine her something she could not pay. I would fine her an amount she could pay. I said I would fine her $100 and asked her when she could pay that. She said two weeks. I gave her a month, but I warned her that if she could not, she needed to call the court to say she needed more time. No more hiding and wishing things would go away.

The expression "burying your head in the sand" refers to the common but mistaken belief that ostriches bury their heads in the sand when frightened to avoid being seen. Avoiding a problem and hoping that it will eventually go away on its own only prolongs the inevitable. I promised this young woman that I would help her get a new start. But in return, she had to share in this responsibility. It was her life that she needed to get back on track.

Once she left my courtroom, I did not hear from her again. It was my hope that she would use this opportunity to take her head out of the sand and learn to deal with small issues before they become big problems.

I do not know if she changed her behavior, but it is never too late to change yours.

CHAPTER 38

Respect Is Valuable

There has never been an older generation that did not complain about how young people behave, about the way they dress, or wear their hair, or how they speak. There has never been an older generation that didn't feel that the younger generations were not sufficiently respectful toward their elders. That is normal, and I understand it.

However, while there may be some generational bias in this observation, when I encountered young people in my courtroom, I hoped to share with them the skills to help them succeed in the world—a world that is often run not by their peers or by their standards, but by those who, for lack of a better word, are part of the establishment.

Many young people today do not seem to know the basic rules of communication to officials, bosses, and to people whose approval they need in one way or another.

So, in my courtroom, when I asked someone to respond to me by saying, "Yes, sir," or "No, sir," it was not about showing me respect; it was asking them to show respect to the legal process and my role in it. Knowing and observing the basic rules of etiquette has always been essential for anyone who wants to make a good impression, not only in the courtroom but everywhere in life.

Someone who replies, "Yep" or even "Yeah," rather than "Yes" or "Yes, sir" or "Yes, ma'am" is sending a message that they are indifferent or do not care about their situation. That is never a recipe for success, in life or in court.

Let me share an example: a young woman, Kaitlyn, had gotten a ticket for running a yellow light in her father's car. She appeared in court with her father, Edmond, who wanted her to take responsibility for the ticket. I asked her what her defense was. She offered up that she was late for school and thought she could make the light.

The video of the incident showed that she had only been three tenths of a second late, which in my courtroom meant her ticket was going to be dismissed.

Kaitlyn told me she was a student at Rhode Island College, studying to be an elementary or secondary school teacher. She was a sweet young woman with a great smile, a sense of humor, and a positive attitude, but when asked questions, she answered, "Yeah" or "Yup"—there was no "Yes, sir," or "Yes, your honor." She was also, I detected, chewing gum as she spoke.

She still had a lot to learn about decorum in court or speaking in a professional setting.

"When you are in a situation where you are before an authority," I explained to her, "you address people by their title, or by the court's title. It's 'Yes, your honor,' not 'Yeah.'" And I also told her that when I was a kid, if you were found chewing gum in class, the teacher made you put the gum on your nose.

She laughed, but she understood my point. And I hoped she would pass along these lessons on decorum and the proper way to address figures of authority to her students.

That was just one of the ways I advised young people to smarten up.

Respect comes in many forms: how you look, how you talk, your attitude, even the friends you choose, reflect on you and the impression you make on others. It is also a way to show self-respect.

I will also note that our middle-aged and older generations seem to have lost a sense of duty about modeling this behavior and passing it down. In today's world there seems to be a widespread reluctance to play the role of mentor, to step up and speak up for what you know is right. People are afraid to tell a younger person to behave in a respectful manner for fear of a confrontation. And they are wise to do so, because we live in an increasingly violent world.

However, the only way to have a civil society is if each of us models that behavior and encourages those we know to do the same.

When young people appeared before me in court, I also often tried to convey the importance of showing up for others and being engaged citizens. It is more than a matter of showing respect for our system of government; it shows a willingness to work to make a better world.

Too many people today have soured on politics and do not believe they can have an impact on their community. We need to find ways to have our children learn the value of acts of service to their neighborhoods, communities, cities, states, nation, and the world.

One method I've considered and put to the test is to encourage young people to become more involved in civic life by having them perform community service rather than paying a fine. On the one hand, it is a reminder of the penalty for being inattentive to the traffic laws and parking regulations. On the other hand, it is my sincere hope that young people will see how doing community service makes a positive difference in their community, and also makes a positive difference in them.

For example, Camilla Cabella was a young woman who appeared in my courtroom. She came to court with her father, who said he was there as emotional support. She had received a violation that she was hoping to get dismissed.

Rhode Island's good driving statute provides that any person who has had a driver's license for more than three years, and who has not been charged with a traffic violation within the preceding three years, may move to have the charged traffic violation dismissed. However, Camilla was still six months shy of the three-year mark.

I asked what she did. She told me she was a student at the University of New Hampshire, studying environmental engineering. I asked her what her dream job would be, and she told me that her dream was to work for under-resourced communities providing them with clean water. She told me that in her next year at college she wanted to join the campus organization Engineers Without

Borders to volunteer her time. She had not been able to do so last year because she was diagnosed with multiple sclerosis and had to spend a lot of time at home.

I could tell that Camilla was a young woman who wanted to do good in the world. I told her father that he had reason to be proud of his daughter and that she had impressed me with her sense of purpose and her very genuine personality.

I ended up dismissing the charge with the promise from Camilla that at some future time she would do ten hours of community service of her choice, something I could tell she was going to do even without my asking her.

The more young people like her there are in the world, the better our world will be.

CHAPTER 39

Politics

Today politics has a bad connotation. Too often, politics now seems to divide us when the purpose of politics should be to engage our citizens in the lifeblood of our communities, cities, states, and nation.

Let me make an argument that you may find outdated or irrelevant to your life. Politics shows a level of respect. Whether it is respect for our system of government, the political process, or specific issues, politics is the process by which change, mostly for the better, occurs.

Today, our political environment has become so fractious, and the rhetoric so dismissive and insulting, that it is easy to forget our nation's achievements at every level of government. The many freedoms and privileges that we take for granted, people in other countries are suffering for not having them. Beyond that, politics can be fun, filled with people who are blessed for a short while with prominence, and even fame.

The price of entry into local politics is something anyone can afford. It is free when you volunteer for a local campaign. It is a great way to meet new people, make lifelong and sometimes important friends, and establish relationships that can serve you well.

For many years, I was involved in politics. I first served as a councilman in Providence when I was quite young. Over the years I worked my way up the ladder of the Rhode Island Democratic Party and was part of the Rhode Island delegation to many Democratic National Presidential Conventions from 1964 to 2012. Eventually,

At the Federal Hill Democratic campaign
headquarters with neighbors, circa 1966

I went as vice chair of the delegation, which was exciting. I would have a bunch of passes to the convention at my disposal, which I would usually distribute each morning to the delegates and other dignitaries. Floor passes were highly sought after and difficult to get if you were not an elected delegate.

In 1976, the convention was in New York City at Madison Square Garden. I went to the convention as vice chair of the Rhode Island delegation, along with Frank Licht, the former governor of Rhode Island. Because it is only a three-hour drive or train ride from Providence to New York City, a lot of people from Rhode Island came down, and they all wanted floor passes to get into the Garden. Though I had given away many passes, eventually I had to say, "I don't have any more. See if you can talk to the governor; he's got the passes."

But I had kept two floor passes. I just did not know who I was going to give them to. Based on experience, I knew that the right situation, or people, would present themselves.

It was about halfway through the floor session when I left the Garden. The organizers had set up a red carpet and had all these wooden barriers on both sides to keep back the crowds of people, all of whom were hoping to see the politicians and celebrities—movie stars, TV journalists, the influencers of their day—who were present.

As I walked out, I saw two young people who were college students. They were holding hands, leaning over the police barrier, and looking at everyone coming and going as if it were the Academy Awards. Something drew me toward them, so I walked over and said, "You want to get into the convention?"

"Could we, could we?"

I said, "See these passes? These are floor passes. You're going to go right down on the floor."

"Oh my God! Oh my God!" they squealed with delight.

"Nobody can stop you because these passes are certified," I said. "Just don't tell anybody who gave them to you."

I watched as the students ran into Madison Square Garden. Suddenly, they stopped, turned around, and said, "Thank you! Thank you!"

To me, that was worth the whole convention. There is nothing like the feeling of making someone's day. Try it sometime, if you never have. Surprise someone with something delightful and notice how it makes you feel.

Conventions, of course, are their own reality show, and the power and the status of politicians can sometimes make people treat the candidates as if they were not just human like the rest of us. It's not so much that it all goes to the candidates' heads (although that has been known to happen); it's that the people around them get swollen heads.

In 1984, we were in San Francisco when Walter Mondale was the nominee. He was a U.S. senator from Minnesota and the former vice president of the United States, under President Jimmy Carter, from 1976 to 1980.

We stayed in the same hotel as Mondale. He was in the penthouse suite. Every time he left the hotel, they locked down the place. There was a car waiting with Secret Service protection and police cars in front and behind them. They moved in a pack; it seemed like there were always twenty people surrounding Mondale. You could not take the elevators until he went down, got in the car, and was driven away.

Everyone was focused on the nominee. Everyone would ask, "Where's the nominee?" Somebody would say, "I saw his daughter; she was walking the dog," or somebody would say, "I caught a glimpse of him as he was walking away." The nominee was so important.

Fast-forward four years. This time we were in Atlanta, Georgia, for the 1988 convention, and we were getting on a crowded elevator. A tall man was already inside, and everyone in our group was asking him to stand back to make room for us. He did, and when we got off the elevator, I asked my two sons who were with me, "Do you know who that was?" They had no idea. I told them that it was George McGovern, who had been the nominee in 1972. Back then they would shut down the hotel when he came and left, and McGovern had police and Secret Service protection. People were excited to just get a glimpse of him. However, in 1988, no one recognized him, no one remembered him, and people were pushing him to the back of the elevator.

Now let's fast-forward twenty years, to the 2008 Democratic Convention in Denver that would nominate Barack Obama. The way that conventions work is that sometimes if you are lucky or from a big state, you get put in hotels close to all the action. But, reflecting our status as a small state, the hotel for the Rhode Island delegation was more than twenty minutes outside of downtown. So, we had to go back and forth and allow for commuting time.

At the end of the convention, as we readied to leave the hotel, we were loading our bags into a car to go to the airport. There was a car parked behind us, and soon enough two gentlemen came out of the hotel, wheeling their bags to the car. It was only after the men put their bags in the trunk, got in the car, and drove off that I realized that the older man was Walter Mondale. Now part of the Minnesota delegation, he was staying in the same hotel as Rhode Island's, stuck in this far-from-the-action place, hauling his own luggage, and driving his own car. It was a far cry from the treatment he received in 1984 as nominee, but I give Vice President Mondale a lot of credit for still giving back to our country by remaining involved in politics and doing so without the attention and fanfare and any of the trappings of power.

I watched as Mondale drove away in his car, and then turned to my sons and said, *"Sic transit gloria."* Fame is fleeting.

CHAPTER 40

Make Yourself Useful

Sometimes respect is serving others selflessly, which is often fundamental to politics. And sometimes politics becomes more than a living—it becomes a life.

I've spoken earlier of my failed 1970 campaign to become Rhode Island Attorney General. At that time, I had already served eight years on the Providence City Council, and I had ambitions for higher office.

The campaign started off well with the polls showing I was ahead. There was no doubt in my mind I was going to win. However, I did not run a good campaign. We had hired two political consultants from Boston who had run some high-level campaigns, but they didn't understand Providence.

Nonetheless, there were some memorable funny moments. One time, we had decided to hold a rally in downtown Providence to which we brought a live donkey as symbol of the Democratic party. After the rally, we had to get the donkey back into the pickup truck. The problem was, we didn't know how to make a donkey, who was as stubborn as you might imagine, climb back into the truck. We were stumped about what to do.

It started to become a spectacle. The donkey just wouldn't move. I was afraid that the press would get a hold of this, and the next day I would wake up to the headline, "Donkey Makes an Ass out of Caprio Campaign."

Then Tup had an idea. He marched the donkey into a warehouse building and out to its loading dock. Then we pulled the truck to the dock, dropped the rear guard, and the donkey just walked onto the flatbed.

So, we may have lost the election, but we had fun. But that's not the point of this story. More importantly, it was during that campaign for attorney general that I met one of my best friends.

At the time I was in my early thirties, and one day this fourteen-year-old kid named Mark Weiner showed up to volunteer. Mark lived with his parents and sister in an apartment in downtown Providence. He was a frumpy-looking teenager with thick glasses, who had flat feet and shuffled when he walked. But he had a soft voice, a kind soul, and boundless energy.

Everybody who met Mark loved him. Even at fourteen years old, he had a natural connection with people, a trait that would serve him well in politics and in life.

Mark had so much energy, all in the service of the campaign. No job was too small; he always asked, "What can I do to help?" There was no ego involved.

During that campaign Mark fell in love with politics, and after my campaign, he worked on many other campaigns both at the

Mark Weiner walked into the headquarters and never left.
Here he is, circa 1973, with my children on his back.

local and the national level. Mark was a great example of how tire-
lessly serving others, showing them respect and earning respect for
doing so, could not only make a difference for a candidate and a
future administration, but also provide someone with a meaningful life, and a lot of fun.

In the lead-up to the 1976 presidential contest, a Democrat was going
to have to face Gerald Ford, a president who had not been voted in
by an election but who became president because Richard Nixon had
resigned. Ford had pardoned Nixon, and the country was not ready

to forgive him for that. Besides, it was time for a change, so it looked good for the Democratic candidate, whoever it would be.

At the time, the front runner was Henry "Scoop" Jackson, a Democratic senator from the state of Washington who leaned to the right on military matters and foreign affairs but who was also a champion of human rights and the environment. He had won important primaries in New York and Massachusetts. He was running against Frank Church, an Idaho senator who had come to prominence during the Watergate hearings, and Jimmy Carter, a former peanut farmer who was governor of Georgia.

I was chairman of the Rhode Island delegates for Scoop Jackson. He was the favorite in the Rhode Island primary, but, unfortunately, he withdrew from the race prior to our primary election day. So, we now had a number of uncommitted delegates. Mark and I went to speak to Joe Paolino, who had served with me on the Providence City Council and would go on to become the mayor of Providence and U.S. ambassador to Malta, about what to do. We had heard that Jerry Brown, the governor of California, was thinking of running and that he was in Baltimore.

Mark said to me, "I'll get his number and call him and see if he's interested in the support of our uncommitted delegates."

We reached Jerry Brown on the phone. We explained that we had these uncommitted delegates and that if he came to Rhode Island, we would endorse him, and he would win the Rhode Island primary. "It's too late to have my name on the ballot," Brown said. "You'd have to tell people to vote 'UNC' (uncommitted) and that their vote will be a vote for Jerry Brown. That will never happen."

Mark, Joe, and I convinced Brown that if he came to Rhode Island, it would happen. Back then, presidential candidates rarely came to Rhode Island, the smallest state. We knew that Brown's presence in Rhode Island would be a major local media event. More importantly, the people of Rhode Island would take notice and connect with the candidate who took the time to visit our state. So, he came, and we spent a few days with him.

Brown, as governor of California, one of the largest states in America, was used to campaigning by holding rallies and using TV ads and press coverage to get his message out. We told him that was not how it worked in Rhode Island. Instead of stadiums, we went to bowling alleys and other places where people congregated. We got a van, and we drove him around to weddings and other functions, since at that time it was not uncommon for people to invite 400 people to their wedding. We were the original wedding crashers. We went to popular venues around Rhode Island and even to Massachusetts locations where many Rhode Islanders held their celebrations.

Brown was not familiar with Rhode Island–style retail politics and kept saying, "I don't do this." We promised that if he followed our advice, we would win Rhode Island for him. It was not easy because his name was not on the ballot. We had to convince

Campaigning for Jerry Brown

people to vote for "Uncommitted." But we did it. "Uncommitted" on behalf of Jerry Brown won Rhode Island, in what was an upset victory—and perhaps the only time a candidate won the state without having his name on the ballot. It only happened because Jerry Brown trusted Mark, Joe Paolina, and me.

Jerry Brown was a very intelligent, seasoned politician who had already won elections and achieved great things in California. Despite all this, and the fact that he was launching a national presidential campaign, Brown quickly realized that he did not know Rhode Island politics. He respected that we did, and we delivered—and I'm not sure we could have, or would have, without the respect we had for him, and the respect he showed us.

Jerry Brown never amassed enough delegates nationally to be a serious contender, and the day after Brown ended his presidential campaign, Mark traveled to Georgia to see how things were going at Jimmy Carter's headquarters. In typical Mark fashion, he just walked in. And he stayed, asking, "What can I do?" There were rumors, likely true, that for a while he even slept on the floor there. Hamilton Jordan, who at the age of twenty-six had run Carter's successful campaign for Georgia governor and was now a key advisor, took a liking to Mark.

During Carter's presidential campaign, Mark's career flourished. Mark was one of the many young people who traveled around the country supporting Carter in all the primary states leading up to the national election. Once Carter had secured the Democratic nomination, Mark, now college-age, was sent by the campaign to wherever he was needed. So, for example, Mark worked closely with the person who was running Carter's campaign in Indiana, a woman who had just gotten married the month before and was now known by her married name, Hillary Rodham Clinton.

After the election, Mark went to the White House, pretty much at his own invitation. No one quite knew what he did. But Mark did what Mark did best: he made himself useful. He created his own job. Mark was involved in getting people to events. If someone wanted tickets to visit the White House, Mark handled it. And if someone at the White House wanted to attend an event in D.C., say a sporting event, Mark arranged that. It was a job no one else wanted, but he saw the value in it. Everyone else was trying to curry favor, but Mark was doing favors for important people and making amazing friends and contacts everywhere.

In 1980, Mark decided to put his political savvy, connections, and general fandom to good use by creating Financial Innovations (now F.I.I.), a Rhode Island firm that served as the official merchant and supplier of banners, pens, hats, and countless other items used in Democratic political campaigns and at every Democratic National Convention since then.

In 1988, Mark was selling political merchandise at the Democratic National Convention in Atlanta, and my son Frank stopped by his office at the convention hall to try to get an extra pass to the convention. As he was asking for Mark, Jimmy Carter walked in, looking for an extra pass. Here was the former president of the United States in his home state, and he was going to Mark for passes. That was who Mark was.

Fortunately, Mark was able to get passes for both of them. I pressed Mark later that day as to what he would have done if he only had one extra pass. Who would have gotten it? He assured me that it would have gone to Frank, and I absolutely believed him!

Mark became close to Bill Clinton when Clinton was governor of Arkansas, and he remained close to Bill and Hillary during the Clinton presidency, and when Hillary ran for U.S. Senate and later became Secretary of State. Mark was one of the people Bill and Hillary called when they just wanted to talk to a friend.

One time, during the Clinton presidency, Mark called me to ask where I was watching the Duke versus University of Connecticut basketball game. I told him I was planning to watch it at home. Mark asked, "How'd you like to watch it at the White House with the President?" I said I'd love to.

So off to Washington I went. There were only about fifteen of us watching the game. I was sitting next to William Cohen, the Secretary of Defense. Hillary and Chelsea were out of the country at the time.

After the game was over, the President gave us a tour of the Rose Garden, pointing out certain trees that were gifts from certain countries and the wheelchair ramp that had been installed for FDR. Then he invited us to join him in the Oval Office.

Now it was just Mark and me and four other people. It was probably one of the most exhilarating experiences in my life. Clinton had a photographic memory, and he could recall details of every book in his personal library. There were many mementos there.

Clinton explained that he had chosen for his desk "the Resolute," whose wood was taken from a U.S. frigate. He had recently installed a new carpet in the Oval Office. He asked me to compare the Presidential seal on the Resolute desk with the seal on the carpet. I couldn't see any difference, but Clinton pointed out that the American eagle had arrows in one set of its talons and olive branches in the other. On the Resolute, the eagle was looking at the arrows; on the carpet it was looking at the olive branches. Clinton explained that until Harry S. Truman's presidency the eagle looked at the arrows, but after World War II, Truman changed it so that the eagle looked at the olive branches—so that the United States was no longer thought of as a warmongering nation.

After the Clinton presidency, Bill often invited Mark to travel the world with him. Bill and Mark would play cards until all hours, laugh, and talk about their families. Titles, wealth, power, fame—Mark didn't care about any of that. He respected others and saw the true humanity in people, which was very comforting to everyone he met. He was the most loyal friend you could ever have.

In 2016, despite valiantly battling health issues, Mark was planning to go to Philadelphia for the Democratic National Convention. On July 26, 2016, Mark woke up early to prepare to travel to Philadelphia. He was very much looking forward to hearing his friend Hillary Clinton become the first female nominee from a major party on the evening of July 28. Mark then went back to bed for a nap before he planned to head out. He never woke up again; he had passed away. He was only sixty-two.

Bill Clinton spoke at the convention that night, describing how he and Hillary met. "She laughed that big laugh of hers and I thought, well, heck, since my cover has been blown, I asked her to take a walk down to the art museum," Bill recalled. "We have been walking, and talking, and laughing together ever since." Here, he also saw fit to inform the world about Mark's passing. "And we have done it in good times, through joy and heartbreak. We cried together this morning on the news that our good friend and a lot of your good friend, Mark Weiner, passed away early this morning."

They stopped the campaign for a day to attend Mark's funeral in Providence. Bill delivered a eulogy for him, as did I. It was one of toughest things I ever had to do. Bill, Hillary, I, and almost everyone in attendance openly cried that day.

I miss Mark, but I carry his spirit with me, always. There was never a day when I did not respect Mark as a human being, and not a day when I didn't feel he respected me.

Value your friends dearly and tell them how much they mean to you. You never know when you will lose one. We all should be so lucky to have a person like Mark Weiner in our lives.

CHAPTER 41

Accidents Are Opportunities

When our older children started to be school-aged, Joyce and I moved to Narragansett, a quiet seaside town about forty miles from Providence. There was a hotel a few miles from our house called the Dutch Inn that had an indoor swimming pool where Joyce would take the kids on winter days for some fun. There was also a bar area with pinball machines that the kids liked to play.

One time, my son David was playing on a pinball machine when he ran out of quarters. My wife gave him a dollar bill to change at the bar. In his ten-year-old enthusiasm, he ran through the bar area to the reception, which had an open glass sliding door.

However, when he ran back, he did not realize that someone had closed the door. He ran right through the glass door, causing him to bleed profusely from his head.

I was in Providence at work, thirty-four miles away. Joyce was understandably very upset when she called me, so I jumped in my car and rushed there. By the time I arrived, it was clear that, although he had a small cut on his forehead, miraculously, he was fine. But the manager there, Jim Kelso, was very worried because everyone had told him that David's father was a lawyer. He was concerned that I was going to sue him.

Once I saw that David was okay, I sought out Jim, who was so nervous that I told him to sit down, and I bought him a drink at his own bar. We got to talking, and I told him how much I appreciated that the hotel and the pool were an oasis for the kids in the winter.

Jim liked my attitude and said, "Why don't we have breakfast tomorrow morning?" And we did. He was just such an upbeat person, a decent guy, very bright and equal parts crazy, but in an endearing way. He was the classic old-school restaurateur. He was everybody's friend, the person you wanted to sit next to when you walked into a bar where you didn't know anyone. He was full of entertaining stories from the restaurant business and his life experience. Although we had just met, it felt like we were already lifelong friends, which we became over the next few months.

One day he told me that he had been approached by Joe Formicola, a smart young real estate broker who had good instincts and hospitality experience, about buying a shuttered local restaurant in Narragansett called the Coast Guard House. He explained that he wanted me to be part of the deal.

The place was a complete wreck. Here was this beautiful and historic venue on the Atlantic Ocean, literally almost on the water. However, the kitchen faced the ocean, and the bar faced the street. The windows were old crank-style windows, and they were set up so high that you needed to be at least six feet tall to see the ocean.

Jimmy, however, saw that the key to making the Coast Guard House a success was having not just great food, which certainly was a priority, but also, given the restaurant's location, an outdoor deck on the second floor with a bar that served light food. Jimmy believed that was going to be our profit center. He was right.

Jimmy knew the entire restaurant business: how to run the kitchen and how to run the bar. Joe knew real estate and the hospitality business, and I helped with legal, zoning, and permits as the attorney on the team. We each made important contributions, which made for a great partnership.

With my close friend and business partner Jim Kelso

With my current Coast Guard House partners, Bob
Leonard (*left*) and Joe Formicola (*right*)

Over the years, the restaurant withstood several storms and
hurricanes, including Hurricane Bob in 1991, Hurricane Irene in
2011, and Superstorm Sandy in 2012. Each time, the bar was dam-
aged and each time we rebuilt and remodeled, so much so that we
could finally reconfigure the entire restaurant to the way it should
have been all along. The bar is now on the ocean and the views are
breathtaking. I've had the good fortune to travel the world and can
objectively say there is not a better water view anywhere. The din-
ing room has also been completely remodeled, and the kitchen is
state of the art. It is now a nationally recognized restaurant.

I am lucky to have had both Jimmy and Joe in my life. They
were great partners, as was Debbie, Jimmy's wife, who assumed his

role after Jimmy died in 1999. In 2000, Bob Leonard and his wife, Alyssa, a top sommelier, acquired an ownership interest. As managing partners, they played a major role in transforming the restaurant into what it is today.

I have been very fortunate. But it is important to note that I've been open to being fortunate. I have often said that it's a lot of work to be lucky. What I mean by that is that when you put yourself out there with an open heart and a positive mindset, the world comes to you with untold possibilities. For example, that day, my only concern as I rushed to Narragansett was my son's health. I was never looking to blame anyone. That so surprised Jimmy, the manager there, that what might have been a confrontation turned into an adventure where I became part of something that changed my family's life for the better.

In other words, as someone else put it: "When opportunity knocks, be sure you are ready to walk through the door."

I am very proud of the operation at the Coast Guard House. Although we have a full professional staff, in the summer we hire anywhere from 130 to 150 college students to work as servers, dishwashers, bus staff, chefs, cooks, and security. We have employed thousands of youngsters. Many come back to see us as they progress in their lives; some have become extremely successful in their professional lives, and they talk about the importance of having worked at the restaurant. They made enough money to help them in their education and their future endeavors. And just like in sports, they learned the value of being part of a team and working hard.

All this good for so many people over so many years came from one simple impulse: rather than seeking to sue someone, I sat down with Jim Kelso, and we got to know each other. Rather than be accusatory or defensive, we showed each other respect.

What we discovered was that we had more we could accomplish together than we ever would have from one small lawsuit, which could have cost a person his job and his family their livelihood.

CHAPTER 42

Respect for Our Veterans

The Coast Guard House restaurant was originally built as a lifesaving station in 1888. Nonetheless, its very name triggers an association with our Coast Guard and the military forces that defend our nation. Those who served our nation need to be remembered for their service. I am proud that in my years on the bench in Providence many veterans appeared in my courtroom, and I was able to express my, as well as the entire court's, gratitude to them.

Into my courtroom came veterans who had fought in World War II, in Korea or Vietnam, and in our more recent wars in Iraq, Kuwait, and Afghanistan.

The most memorable veteran who ever appeared in my courtroom was Caster Salemi, who had served in World War II. Caster was the personification of the Greatest Generation. He was extremely modest about his service but told the court that he served in the U.S. Army from 1943 to 1946 in the Pacific theater. He served one year in New Guinea, where his troop made preparations to land in Luzon to expel the Imperial Japanese forces occupying the Philippines. He also fought in the Philippines for a year. He was with the troops at Bataan, and they were set to liberate Manila but, Caster said, "that city was already destroyed when we arrived."

He was in Luzon when the war ended, but that was not the end of his service. He was tasked with gathering all the Japanese nationals and transferring them to Manila for repatriation.

Fast-forward some sixty years later, and Caster was in my court for having run a red light. He told us he had just turned 100, and he had been driving for eighty-four years without a ticket. The courtroom applauded him for his service, and for his 100 years.

"You represent people who respect one another and cover for one another, who protect others," I told him. "We can never ever thank you and your generation enough for the contributions you made for this country. You really did make the world safe, and we want to thank you and honor you for your service and your bravery.

"This case is dismissed," I told him. I wanted to do the honorable thing for this honorable man.

On another occasion, an older gentleman named Roland Gavin appeared in my courtroom. He had received a ticket for parking in a prohibited zone. Roland told me that he had indeed parked at the location but, as a former police officer, he had checked for "No Parking" signs—there were none—and even checked whether the curb was painted red or yellow—it was not. There was no indication it was a prohibited zone, so he had parked there.

Inspector Carignan and I were inclined to believe him, so we dismissed the ticket. As Roland was about to leave the courtroom, he mentioned that he was a Vietnam War veteran. I asked him back to the podium.

"You didn't tell us you were a Vietnam vet," I said.

"You didn't ask," was his quick reply. We all laughed. It turned out Roland had served three years in Vietnam and was on the USS *Enterprise* when it blew up off the coast of Hawaii. "I lost twenty-eight of my men on that day," he said.

I told him that I have a particular soft spot for Vietnam veterans. The Vietnam War was a very unpopular war. We fought a losing battle against guerrilla forces and eventually withdrew in a chaotic fashion. Many Vietnam vets returned with physical injuries, as well as emotional and psychological ones. There is a disproportionate number of Vietnam vets who became addicts or homeless, or both. At the time, not everyone understood what they went through, and those veterans were treated as the representatives of a war policy many found wrong. When they returned home, instead of being welcomed as heroes, instead of being appreciated for the sacrifices they made for our country, they were often treated with anger and hostility.

"That's why," Roland said, "anytime we see a veteran that's in uniform, we go up to him and we thank him for his service. Because we didn't get that when we came back."

Another case involving a Vietnam veteran that touched me was that of Richard Eaton. Richard had run a red light. He had never received a ticket before. He explained that he was returning from the VA hospital where he had just received a shot, and perhaps he was not paying full attention.

As a teenager, Richard attended East Providence High. Immediately after graduation, he was drafted and served from 1969 to 1971 in Vietnam.

I shared with Richard that during the Vietnam War I was teaching high school and going to law school at night, and I was coaching the high school wrestling team. "One of my wrestlers was the nicest kid you've ever met in your life. His name was Andrew Jackson, just like the former president. He was a gentleman, he was a great kid, and immediately upon graduation, he enlisted, and he went to Vietnam," I said. "And four months later, he was dead. I never forgot that. And it just bothered me, and it bothered me that veterans returning from Vietnam were not given the respect they deserved."

What I decided to do in Richard's case was to also dismiss his ticket. However, I wanted to first read a letter I received from Honolulu, Hawaii, from a gentleman named Greg Abe: "My father served in World War II with the 447-combat-regimental-team and he still knows to have compassion for everyone. He says, 'Every chance I get, I thank every veteran I see. At times I even pay for their meals anonymously.'" I told Richard that there was a man in Hawaii who wanted to give back to someone who had served in the military, so he sent in a check for $30 made payable to the court.

"I'm going to dismiss your case and we are going to honor Mr. Abe, who is a teacher at Roosevelt High School in Honolulu. We're going to charge you $30 court costs and use Mr. Abe's check to pay that and to honor him and his father's service." That seemed like the fitting thing to do. I will just mention that the episode with Richard Eaton touched a chord in the hearts of people all over the world, as it has had more than 100 million views.

Only about one third of the men and women who served in Vietnam are still alive today. If you happen to meet one of them, please thank them for their service—it's well deserved and long overdue. I also encourage everyone to support veterans' organizations. These organizations are always in need of contributions and volunteers.

CHAPTER 43

Diversity Works

There are many ways to serve your community, your city, your state, and your nation and be an agent of change. I was reminded of this when Lawrence Wilson III came before me regarding an overdue ticket for running a red light and for three parking tickets.

Lawrence was tall and good-looking, with a very open, friendly, and relaxed manner. He mentioned that he had been at the mayor of Providence's inauguration and had seen me swear in the mayor on the steps of City Hall. He recalled it was a freezing day, which it had been.

At first, I kidded with him that what he should have said to me was not about the temperature that day but what a great job I did swearing in the mayor. Laughing, I asked him if he wanted to start over again.

"Yes, your honor," he said. "You were terrific!" Now we were both laughing.

I asked Lawrence why he had been at the mayor's inauguration. "I've supported him, and I've worked with him," he explained. Then he went on to tell me that he had started a new firm called Leadership and Diversity (later renamed the Wilson Organization) that helps companies become more diverse, more representative of the populations they serve, and he had worked with the mayor on this issue.

Over time, Lawrence would appear three times before me regarding parking tickets. He did not avoid them, and when he gave credible explanations, those tickets were dismissed. And whenever fines were dismissed, he donated the amounts he would have been liable for to local charities, and those donations were matched by the Filomena Fund.

I would like to commend him for promoting leadership and diversity within the Providence business community. Embracing diversity is the first step toward not just tolerance but true understanding and acceptance of others.

Embracing diversity is just another way of showing respect to others. We have so much to learn from others who can bring their own perspective and insights to the full range of customer-, consumer-, and client-facing businesses. And that includes the law as well.

As the American business leader Malcolm Forbes once said, "Diversity is the art of thinking independently together." In today's global environment, embracing diversity is not just a virtue but a requirement for survival, not just for businesses but for communities and countries as well.

Making companies more diverse and having better representation may seem like a no-brainer. But in truth, there is often resistance when you are trying to change the status quo. As I have mentioned several times now, I have personally felt excluded based solely on my Italian heritage. I have the battle scars. I can only imagine what it must be like to be discriminated against due to the color of your skin or your gender.

First, for many, many years, corporations and government officials didn't even know they had a problem. They thought, "This is the way it is." Or worse, "This is the way it has always been, and will always be."

Then, the next thing you always hear—and I heard this about Italians when I was growing up—"We would hire them, but we can't find a good candidate." Whatever the minority, the answer was always: "They don't have the training, they don't have the experience. We can't find qualified candidates to hire."

However, this is putting the cart before the horse. What makes the work of Lawrence Wilson so critical is that to hire diverse candidates, companies need to recruit them, train them, and bring in competent candidates from other industries. We need to look at the barriers to entry and question if they are so important. If the candidate can do the job well, do they need to have a college or advanced degree? If they need a degree, can we help them get that degree while they are working? These are the questions we should be asking.

Diversity is important for so many reasons, not the least of which is that children need to see people who look like them in positions of authority, competence, and excellence.

According to the Providence public schools' own website, "combined, our students and families speak fifty-five different languages and hail from ninety-one countries of origin," which can make it challenging for students to learn. But one day, one of those children may be our next mayor, governor, or even president.

My courtroom was a microcosm of the city of Providence, a progressive city that's been welcoming immigrants for hundreds of years. Many of the defendants who have appeared before me may not have felt life had treated them fairly, but it was my sincere hope that in my courtroom they felt they had the opportunity to speak, to be heard, and to be treated fairly in the way our system of justice demands. If they didn't feel that on the way into the courtroom, I hope they felt so on the way out.

CHAPTER 44

Know Your True Value

O ne facet of self-respect that I had to learn was to know your true value and ask for it.

Richard, the friend I met through his divorce, was the person who taught me to get paid for the things that I used to naturally do for free. "You do this stuff every day, and you don't realize the value you are providing." His advice had a profound impact on my business and personal life.

One example occurred when my law associate had met a real estate professional who wanted to build a 160-bed nursing home near Providence. As a developer as well, he would oversee the construction, and his partner would be the nursing home administrator. They had all their plans, but they needed to get specific approvals from the Federal Housing Authority (FHA) to qualify for certain federal credits and benefits. They were meeting roadblocks at every turn.

My associate asked if I could help them understand all the approvals they needed. Without dotting all the i's and crossing all the t's, there would be no approval, no deal, and they could not go forward. I looked at the project and thought that it would be a great benefit to the community. I also learned that the woman who was going to be the administrator, Eleanor Pisaturo, was a highly principled, respected, and intelligent professional. That gave me confidence that the nursing home would be successful.

The local FHA administrator was someone I knew, and I was willing to represent this project before her and work to complete and properly submit all the necessary paperwork to get the required approvals. Having been a city councilman in Providence and an attorney in private practice for several years, I had unique insight and experience in how bureaucracies worked and the process by which to get the necessary permits and approvals.

I proposed that if I succeeded, rather than charge a one-time fee, I wanted to be a partner in the deal.

At first, one of the partners refused. "What are you doing that's worth so much?" he asked.

I said it was simple: without me, they could potentially have 100 percent of a deal that was not happening. With me, they could have a somewhat smaller ownership of a project that I would give everything I had to ensure all the administrative and procedural requirements were met. The choice was theirs.

I was asked to leave the room for a moment. Through the doors, I could not hear their conversation verbatim, but I could hear enough shouting to know it was a contentious conversation. At last, the doors opened, and I was invited back in. In short, they agreed to my terms.

I worked through all the documentation required for all the approvals, navigating the process among the various bureaucratic entities. Once we were approved by the FHA administrator, we built Cherry Hill Manor, which is still considered to be the best nursing home in Rhode Island.

It was Richard who taught me this valuable lesson: know the value of what you bring to the table and do not be afraid to ask for it.

I would be remiss if I did not make a special appeal for women to do this. For far too long, women's contributions have been underappreciated and undervalued. For my daughter, nieces, and granddaughters, it is my sincere wish that they are compensated in a manner commensurate with their contributions.

CHAPTER 45

Tough Love

Sometimes, knowing when to say no to people is also a form of self-respect.

Many people thought that as a judge I was too lenient and that I gave breaks to too many of the people who appeared before me in court.

I don't agree with that assessment. I tried to be as compassionate as I could be to people facing difficulties. I strove to understand their circumstances. And when I felt that they and justice were better served by giving them a break, I did so.

However, there were many, many cases in which the person before me had behaved in a way that I could not countenance: they were disrespectful to the clerks at the courthouse, to the court, or to me as judge; or they were flagrant in their disregard of the violations they had incurred, or willfully avoided taking responsibility in ways that made their situation worse. When that happened, I showed less mercy and enforced the law far more strictly.

To me, showing respect and earning respect are all forms of having self-respect. And when you have self-respect, sometimes you have to make the tough decisions about people in your life, who either disrespect you or disrespect themselves in a way that is no longer their problem but yours as well.

We all have our hot buttons, and sometimes in my courtroom there were defendants who managed to push mine. One memorable example involved David Norton.

David came to court to resolve his tickets and problems with his vehicle registrations. He wondered what I could do for him. As I was quick to point out, there was a lot I could do, but the real question was: Why should I?

David had not made much of an effort on his own behalf. His vehicle had been towed, and he already had more than twenty-nine unpaid parking tickets, for a total of $1,090 in fines. He had paid $300, but he still owed the balance on his fines. He had not paid a penny of that. He had instead changed his registration, perhaps thinking no one would know it was the same car. On this new registration, he still got nine more parking tickets.

"There's not a lot of wiggle room here," I told him. His actions concerning his vehicles, which attempted to skirt his responsibilities, had shown complete disrespect to the court. Still, I was not there to persecute him. Rather, I waived some of the extra penalties and had him agree to a payment plan, with a stern warning that if he turned up in my court again there would be no leniency.

Although David did not really help himself by his court appearance, I felt it was appropriate to give him a chance to show some responsibility by implementing a payment plan. If he paid regularly and on time, the total due would be less than the full amount.

However, if he missed a payment, the full fine would be due. It was now up to him to help himself.

⚖

Sometimes the person who came to court was not the one responsible for the ticket, and I loathed to punish the person before me for doing the right thing by showing up.

Maria Lopez came to court about several tickets on her car. It turned out they were all the fault of her son, who was not willing to take responsibility for his actions. He was ready to have his mom bail him out every time. It also turned out her son was twenty-four and had a job. But she still wanted to show up and pay his way.

I suggested it was time for some tough love. I suggested she take the keys away from him. She was unwilling, explaining that her husband had passed away seven years ago, and since then, she could not bring herself to say no to her son.

I understood the sentiment, but the result was no good for either of them.

Being a mom is one of the toughest jobs on the planet, and I hope that Maria's son appreciated all that his mother was doing for him. However, I believe that one of the most important jobs for any parent is to teach their children to take responsibility for their actions. Even a mama bird pushes her young out of the nest to learn to fly on their own.

On the opposite side of the spectrum, there was Yasmin Valdera, whom we called "The World's Strictest Mom." Her twenty-year-old son received one parking ticket while using her car to drive to a new job. She went to the state motor vehicle registry, canceled the registration on the car, and refused to let him drive her other car!

I told her to go home, give him a hug, and say something nice to him. "I do love my kid," she said, "but I'm a single mother and it's not fair. He knows that a parking meter only has so much time. So, pay attention to that so that mom doesn't have to lose my time from work. A $75 ticket for not following the rules, your honor, I don't accept that."

I told her that if a parking ticket was the biggest problem she was having with her son, that she should count her blessings. I dismissed the case based on Yasmin's corrective action prior to coming to court. Her son might not have appreciated what his hardworking, law-abiding single mother did, but I'm confident that he will always have plenty of quarters for the parking meter from now on! He is fortunate to have a mom who understands the importance of providing tough love.

In my courtroom, I also often see young people saddled with the mistakes of their exes who left a mess for them to clean up. I am sorry to say it is mostly women with young children who are suffering the consequences of absent fathers.

On one occasion, medical assistant Tiana Espinal and her three-year-old son, Gabriel, appeared in my court. She also had a sixteen-year-old daughter who was in her senior year at Cranston East High.

She had many tickets. I asked who was responsible for them. She said that some were hers; some were her sister's; and, as the baby's father had registered the car in her name, she was responsible for his tickets as well.

She told me that her husband had left her two months ago. "I'm doing it all by myself," she said. She said she was not getting any money from her ex or from anyone else. I asked her to describe what it was like to be a single mom.

"It's tough," she said. "It's very hard for me." Tiana explained that her daughter was an honor roll student, so she didn't want to give her extra responsibility to help with her brother because she was on track to get a scholarship. Everything fell on Tiana. Her typical day was to drop off her son at Head Start, then go to work. She had to pay her stepdad to pick up her son in the afternoon. After a long day at work, Tiana would pick up her son from her stepdad's place and prepare for the next day. "It's hard because I don't have a break," she said. "But I chose to be a mom."

She was taking care of two children, and I saw that her young son needed her attention. But I was impressed that she maintained a positive attitude and was willing to take responsibility, even when others, like her ex, were not.

Tiana said, "You know why? Because I feel good that I am helping other people. You feel good when you do the right thing."

I felt this dedicated mom, who wanted to help people even when she was the one who needed help, deserved a break. I made sure her fines were paid by the Filomena Fund.

⚖

Another time, a lovely young woman came into my courtroom. She had a ticket for running a red light and four parking tickets. She explained that she shared the car with her boyfriend and that he had gotten the tickets.

I asked her where the boyfriend was this morning. She replied, "He's not here."

I asked why didn't he come to court and "'fess up to this"?

"Because I'm the responsible one," she said.

As I asked her more questions, my heart went out to her. Her boyfriend didn't work. She worked and was also going to school, for which she was paying by herself. All this I applaud. However, I wasn't sure about her choice of companionship. I reduced the fee, but I truly wished her boyfriend would take responsibility.

I hope this young woman sees the light and realizes it's time for her to ditch the dead weight in her life. On occasion, this is exactly what I told the women who came to my courtroom. And, usually, the women would agree with me.

I walk a fine line that's beyond my role as judge. When I see a promising young person who is being taken advantage of, Judge Caprio makes way for my instincts as Papa Caprio, and I offer advice. I hope this young woman took it.

Sometimes people hold back from telling the truth to someone they care for, feeling that it is better that they learn from their own mistakes; or they feel that giving them advice will be taken the wrong way as not showing that person respect. In my experience, the opposite is true—if you care for someone, you show them respect by letting them know that you see the difficulties they are facing and that your life experience suggests a different path for them. If they respect you, they will appreciate the advice, whether they follow it or not.

PART FOUR

Understanding

U nderstanding takes many forms. It is about listening sympathetically and being aware of what another person is feeling. Understanding is a special kind of listening where you are tolerant and forgiving of what they are telling you. It is about letting someone know you truly hear them.

Understanding is also comprehending what you are seeing or being told, whether that is in a foreign language or in English—or even when no words are spoken. It is a certain kind of situational awareness. Understanding means you know what is going on in a given situation.

Finally, and perhaps most importantly, understanding is about having insight—true insight and good judgment about what needs to be done.

In my experience, having compassion will make you a better person. Having respect will deliver dividends in your dealings with others. But you need to have understanding to achieve your full potential as a human being.

On a fundamental level, it means knowing right from wrong and making decisions that allow you to stay on the right path. These are values that are often passed down by your family—which need not be your biological or given family but can be the people who form your safety net—through stories and traditions. These values provide you with a deep understanding of where you come from, and lead to another layer of understanding: Who are you now, and who do you want to be?

If you are not happy with who you are currently, it is never too late to begin being the person you want to be. I believe change is possible; I have seen it occur over and over again. It involves taking responsibility, admitting your mistakes, staying the course, persevering even when a situation seems impossible, and demonstrating that you've learned from your mistakes—these are the behaviors associated with the type of understanding I'm talking about. True understanding means devoting yourself to the truth even when it's hard to face.

Finally, another important component of profound understanding is having a sense of belonging and serving a higher purpose, one that makes us feel part of something larger than ourselves, whether that is in a neighborhood, or a community of faith, or even a charitable organization. What that group is doesn't matter—what matters is having that sense of community that makes life feel meaningful.

CHAPTER 46

Acknowledge Your Mistakes

I am far from perfect. Like all humans, I make mistakes. Over the course of my life, I've made small mistakes, and I've made some big ones. However, when I discover I've made a mistake, I try to acknowledge it. And I am always impressed by people who come to court to acknowledge the mistakes they have made. Acknowledging your mistakes shows that you understand the situation and what you have done, that you have understanding such that you won't do it again.

One time in court I made a mistake. The paperwork I had indicated that Diana Castro, the woman before me, had a car that had been booted, and not for the first time. I was disappointed that she had not learned from her previous mistake, and I felt like she was not being completely honest with me or herself about the situation with her car. I also told her that she had a bad attitude, which further influenced my judgment. As a result, I came down a little hard on her. I levied a big fine, and sent her to the clerk for payment.

As she was going to the clerk, Inspector Quinn quietly informed me that I was incorrect about some of the information I had based my decision on. I didn't realize that she had come to court on her own initiative to try to remedy some outstanding tickets. She had just returned from being out of town due to the death of her grandmother, who had been raising her younger brother. She now had the responsibility of caring for her younger brother and a young child of her own, alone. She came to court to address outstanding tickets so that her car wouldn't be booted.

I was wrong to chastise her. I asked her to come back to court and return to the microphone.

In person, I began by congratulating Diana for voluntarily coming back to court to address her outstanding obligations. I let her know that I thought that her coming to court, as well as her commitment to raising both her brother and her daughter, showed what great strength of character she had. I dismissed most of her tickets and encouraged her to stay strong.

I believe it takes courage to admit you are wrong and to ask for forgiveness. There is no shame in taking the blame, so once again, Diana, please accept my apology, as well as my good wishes for you and your family.

CHAPTER 47

The Road Less Traveled

Occasionally, I encountered people in my courtroom who had followed a bad path in their youth that led them to spend many years in prison for their bad choices. Now adults, they wanted to follow a different path. I support that and always root for them. But when I had the opportunity to have them share what life has taught them so that others, particularly young men, don't make the same mistakes, I encouraged them to do so. Nikita Brown did so, on one memorable occasion.

Nikita came into my courtroom to resolve a summons for a plate on his car that went back twenty years. Twenty years! I asked him where he'd been hiding for the last two decades. What he said surprised me and touched me.

"I've been homeless and messed up in life, trying to get things right and doing all the wrong things. [I've been] in and out of prison, not doing the right things, but finally, I got older and it's different now."

Nikita explained that he was forty-five years old and had spent, in total, almost thirty years behind bars. He had been out of prison now for almost three years.

I told him that he could do a lot of good by talking to young people. I asked him what advice he would give if he were talking to a group of young people who may be showing signs of following the wrong path.

"Honestly, I would tell them that the path that you are about to take, that path is nothing but destruction," he said. "You're not going to get anything good out of it."

I asked him what, in his opinion, was the right path for these kids to follow.

"The right path," he said, "is just be a kid. Don't try to grow up too fast. Just be a kid and do the things that kids do. Don't try to jump into an adult life."

He made a good point. What these kids don't know is that the life they may think of as boring—listening to their parents and elders, staying in school, doing their homework, graduating, and so on—are milestones on the right path.

Speaking with Nikita made me think of Robert Frost's poem "The Road Not Taken," which I quoted to him in part:

Two roads diverged in a wood, and I—
I took the one less traveled by,
And that has made all the difference.

The road less traveled is sometimes boring, or harder, or scarier, but it is often the road of honor and decency, and that makes all the difference. Understanding that can change your life.

I dismissed all his tickets so he could get a driver's license and stay on the good path.

⚒

Sometimes we feel the weight of the world is so great that we can't begin to change our own self-destructive behavior. But I assure you, we can. I believe that a person can change if they truly want that change.

When Steve Dory stepped up to the lectern in my courtroom, I told him that I saw that he had four different car registrations and five tickets in his name—two parking violations from fifteen years ago, two from fourteen years ago, and one speeding ticket from recently. He asked to explain: he only had two vehicles in his name. The other two, he said, "were in another lifetime." I noted there was a large time gap between the violations on the two earlier vehicles and the ones he now owned for which he had come to court.

Steve explained that eight years ago, he had started his road to recovery and that he had been sober now for four years. In the last four years, he had made amends, paid his fines, bought two new vehicles, and bought a restaurant.

"You're a good man," I told him.

"I wasn't always," he admitted.

I told him that I did not see the law as black or white. I understood that people go through crises in their lives. Some people succumb to those crises. Others rise above them. From what I saw, Steve was working hard to rise above his earlier circumstances.

It takes a great deal of courage. It takes a great deal of strength. It takes a great deal of determination.

I know temptation is tough.

I dismissed his tickets from fourteen and fifteen years ago. That left one recent speeding ticket.

Steve explained that it was for speeding in a school zone. But it was Saturday morning at 8 AM and school was not in session.

I dismissed that ticket, too. In truth, I was proud of what Steve had accomplished for himself. Four years sober and owner of his own restaurant, he was building on the new.

He understood, as the world-class gymnast and author Dan Millman wrote, "The secret of change is to focus all of your energy not on fighting the old, but on building the new." Understanding that means nothing is impossible.

CHAPTER 48

A Changed Life

A gentleman who appeared in my court in 2022 said he had appeared before me twenty-two years earlier in 2000.

At the time, he had just gotten out of jail and was in a program at the Salvation Army trying to quit drugs and turn his life around. When he appeared before me that first time, I dismissed all his violations and fines, challenging him to change his life.

Now, two decades later, he told me that our conversation had inspired him to get sober. He stayed sober for eighteen months before he relapsed. In 2009, he was finally able to give up drugs, and he'd been sober since then. He said, "I finally made it."

We know it's not easy. Sobriety, like perfection, is a hard standard to achieve. I saw in my courtroom the terrible impact that addiction has on individuals, families, and society as a whole. As disturbing as that is, it is always worthwhile to encourage people who are maintaining sobriety, hopefully having a positive impact on their efforts. If you take one day at a time, it does add up—and in my courtroom, I saw the successes of people who were eventually able to maintain their sobriety.

On another occasion, a woman named Felicia Muriel proved to be the living embodiment of someone turning their life around. When she came before me, she was seventeen years sober.

Felicia had a parking ticket. I was surprised because her record showed she had never received a parking ticket before. I asked her if she had an explanation.

Felicia said that she received the ticket at Miriam Hospital. Felicia was a recovery coach specialist who was called by the emergency room when someone had been taken to the hospital because they overdosed. "I'm one of the ones that go and try to get someone in [to] detox or treatment." She explained that her organization had an understanding with the valet services at the hospital that allowed them to park at the hospital entrance (which is normally a "no parking" zone) because "time is of the essence." That was where she received the ticket.

I asked Felicia if she could share some of what she does in those situations. "I go in and speak with the person," Felicia said, "and I explain to them where I came from, because I'm coming up on seventeen years of sobriety, so I try to get them to surrender themselves to go into a detox or treatment center." And, Felicia added, "I've been pretty good at it."

Felicia said she was good at her job, and I believed her. I also believed that that by helping others, she continued to help herself. Sober for nearly seventeen years, she had managed to turn her life around and use her past experiences to help others avoid similar pitfalls. She was living a meaningful life, which is the best reward. Felicia was a person who understood her own situation and her own path to recovery, and now she was passing along that understanding to others.

Case dismissed!

CHAPTER 49

Never Give Up

In my courtroom, I saw many people with the weight of the world on them.

Kelly Frutato was a single mom with four children. They had been living in a hotel for three months because their house burned down. Then she received a speeding ticket, and it was because she was rushing to see her dying grandmother.

That's a lot for any one person. As a judge, what was I supposed to do? Make her pay the maximum owed for the ticket? What would that accomplish other than adding to her burden?

You put on the robe. What would you do?

I dismissed the ticket and told Kelly to hang in there, have faith that things will get better, and try to have the strength to hold on until it does.

One morning, a woman named Charlie Douglas came into court. Before we could discuss her tickets, she said to me, "When I was a young kid, I grew up in state care. Governor [Edward] DiPrete and

General Treasurer Anthony Solomon paid for us to get clothes and stuff like that, so I became a really good human being. I became a CNA (certified nursing assistant). I love my job, and I do it really well."

Charlie said that out of all the children she was with in state care, she was the only one who ended up in a good situation. She was placed eventually with a wonderful foster family.

"I was really blessed to go to a home where people really cared. Because [before that] my whole life, they did rotten things to me." She related that at some of the other foster homes "it's not who you are, it's what happens to you." Charlie shared that when she was a young child, one family kept her in a dog cage. While sitting in that cage, she would talk to God, so she never gave up.

She told me she was considering becoming a mentor in her home city of Warren, Rhode Island. I told her that she would make a great mentor because of her lived experience.

"The only thing God gave us," Charlie said, "was kindness . . . we got to be kind to each other."

We talked about what advice she would give young people, and she said to "be still, and not give up hope, because if you stop and listen, what you are looking for will come to you."

I do not have to tell you what I did to her ticket, but I do ask that when you or your children or grandchildren are facing a challenge, tell them about Charlie and how she became an admirable person.

One of the privileges that my job as judge afforded me was the opportunity to meet and occasionally help people who have lived incredibly challenging lives. One woman who appeared before me in court, Yesenia Fernandez, had it tough.

She had five parking tickets from ten years prior for which she never showed up.

"I'm guilty of all the tickets," she said, explaining that her life "is always in a rush."

She said that her mother had kicked her out of the house when she was thirteen, and she'd been staying in different places all over Providence since then. She managed to receive her GED and was now working two jobs. She had been working at the American Automobile Association (AAA) for three years and had left that job to work with adults who have intellectual disabilities living in a group home. She also worked at Dunkin' Donuts on the side. She had two children, boys, nineteen and twelve. She had been living in a shelter, but she was now in an apartment and her children were living with her. She also said that she had been in a relationship where there was domestic violence, which had made her life even more unsteady.

Here was a woman who had been homeless and had been the victim of domestic violence. Yet, despite these hardships, she came to court with an infectious smile, a positive attitude, and a strong desire to get her life back on track. I was truly humbled by her grace and strength of character, and I decided she didn't need ten-year-old parking tickets holding her back. I dismissed those tickets, as well as the overnight parking tickets she had received when she was homeless.

She also had six speeding tickets, three of which were only one mile over the speed limit. I also dismissed those, leaving her with three tickets totaling $250. I was able to apply $100 from the

Filomena Fund, so her fine was reduced to $150, which she could pay over time.

I saw with Yesenia and countless others that there is something cathartic about appearing in court and explaining the circumstances surrounding the infractions. It is more than the mere recitation of facts; it is having someone who is listening. It is about the power of being seen and heard. Many times, when talking about why they received a parking ticket, a person would openly share about their private struggles—and feel better for having done so. It is powerful to witness.

It was an equally powerful experience for me when I saw that my words to someone who became before me in court had an impact. For all its strengths and occasional weaknesses, the American legal system provides a fair and productive process for people to resolve issues and move forward.

Yesenia reminds all of us that the strongest steel is forged in the hottest fires.

CHAPTER 50

Make the Tough Decisions

As I have said before, as a judge, I tried to put myself in the shoes of the defendants who appeared before me and understand the circumstances that led them to be in my courtroom. Sometimes that meant having to tell them the hard truth that they need to make tough decisions about themselves and others.

One example that comes to mind is the case of Mohamed Nazeem, who appeared in my courtroom because he had received two red-light violations.

One of those was an instance when he did indeed run through a red light, but it was at a location where it was not obvious that he had seen the sign prohibiting a right turn on red.

The other incident was much more serious. As we viewed on a video of that incident, not only did Mohammed go through the red light, but another car also almost crashed into him. He was very lucky it was not an accident.

"It was horrible," Mohammed said. But he wanted me to know what was going on that day.

He told me that for many years, since 2011, he had not been working. "I have been battling cancer," he said. "And I thought I was feeling better, so I was driving for Uber." His wife had given him a car phone mount so he would not have to hold his phone while driving. Nonetheless, the car phone mount kept falling off the vent it was in. He explained that it fell right at that moment and that was why he went through the light. He had not been driving fast, and, as soon as he realized what he had done, he stopped.

Mohammed asked me to recognize that running red lights was not in his character and only occurred because after so many years of not working, he wanted to try to work. But he was not going to drive for Uber anymore. "Because I can't do it," he said. "I'm still going through my illness."

I empathized with him, but I had to make sure that he understood that when he ran that red light, he was not only jeopardizing his own safety but that of others. I dismissed the first ticket, but I could not excuse the one in which he had nearly caused an accident. I fined him $85 for the violation and hoped that doing so was the wakeup call he needed to realize that he had not recovered well enough to be able to drive safely.

The decision of when it is time to stop driving is an emotionally charged issue. Driving is so closely tied to independence that the thought of losing that independence keeps many on the road for much longer than is safe for them and the people around them.

You need to understand yourself, and where you are in life, when the time comes to stop driving.

I am at that stage of life, at eighty-seven, when I have to start making those assessments about my own ability to drive safely. Not driving is not the end of life—just a new stage.

If you have a loved one who you do not think should be driving, try to present the issue not as a loss but as a change that requires understanding. Assure them that they have a support system that can help them get where they need so they can remain active, connected, and, most of all, safe.

CHAPTER 51

Use What You Know and Who You Know to Help Others

One of the chapters of my life during which I had a lot of fun, and that most people who know me as a judge don't know about, is the many years I was a fight promoter. I still look back fondly on those days.

It was a family affair. My brother Joe and my son John would film the fights, and my son David and I would announce them. We promoted about twenty fights over a seven-year span.

One of our more memorable fights was in Narragansett. We really hyped this fight. I remember announcing a fight by saying: "It's a real barn burner, the excitement and anticipation has reached a fever pitch. There is electricity in the air."

One of the contenders in that fight came from Rhode Island. His name was Arthur Saribekian, also called the Armenian Assassin, and he really had the ability to become a world champion. He was powerful and knocked out many opponents. He was handsome and in great health. He had a very close-knit family—his father, Robert, especially, would always be at the fights.

However, many years later, I was in court hearing cases and who came in but Arthur Saribekian. I asked him how he was, and his answer was immediate.

"Terrible," he said.

Arthur's was the last case of the day, and afterward, Simon Sarkisian, who works for me and is considered family due to his loyalty, kindness, and dedication, had a chance to speak with him. Their families were both of Armenian heritage and had known each other for decades.

Arthur told Simon that he did not have a job, was homeless, and was sleeping in his car. He said he had no hope.

Arthur, who had been so strong, was now a broken man. It haunted me, and I felt that there had to be something I could do.

So, at Sunday dinner, I asked my family to think about how we could help him.

My brother Joe and my son David took Arthur out to lunch and learned more about his situation. It was clear that Arthur could no longer think clearly and deliberately. The punches to the head seemed to be taking their toll. We talked to his former manager and his boxing coach, who believed that Arthur's career was ruined by an unsavory promoter who used him "as a punching bag" for a heavyweight fighter—and as a result, Arthur took one too many punches.

While Arthur was living in his car and sleeping in it by a local park, he was not drinking or on drugs. He did not have a criminal record, and he wanted to work.

However, the biggest obstacle in his personal life was his broken relationship with his father. After his mother passed away, his father, Robert, let him down. His manager told us, "He's very resentful toward his father and tells people, 'I have no family.'"

We realized that the long-term solution for Arthur was not just financial but also had a lot to do with his family. First, my family would try to help Arthur get a job. He was still physically strong, so he could work. And we would help find him temporary housing, so he didn't have to sleep in his car. Those would not be easy. However, they were simple compared to repairing his relationship with his father. His strength had always stemmed from maintaining his solid family unit. We needed to help him rebuild that.

We began by approaching his father, Robert. Simon sat down with him and asked him: Do you still believe in Arthur? Robert said he did. So, we asked him to come by my office the next day at 5 PM.

Honestly, no person has a magic wand to make things right. There was no guarantee that bringing Arthur and his father together would accomplish anything other than more recriminations and hurt feelings. But it was worth a try.

Arthur's father arrived first. I reminded Robert of how much faith he had had in his son in the past, and I was candid in saying that clearly things had changed.

Robert told me that whenever he talked to Arthur to tell him to get his life together, Arthur was offended.

I explained that I have five kids and I understood how difficult it can be. I told him, "Everybody gets knocked down in life. The question is: Can you get back up?"

When Arthur came into the room, he was surprised to see his father there and was uncomfortable being in the same room with him.

I told Arthur, "Today is the first day of the rest of your life." I asked if there was something, even a small thing, we could do to bring them back on the path to being together.

"When you had nowhere to go," Arthur said to his father, "I took you into my apartment, gave you money, did whatever I had to do. What did you do for me when I needed you?"

Robert was defensive. "You disappear from everyone's life, and you expect me to guess where you live? It's just a shame."

Arthur replied, "You should be ashamed."

They went at each other. I was flabbergasted. I did not dream the animosity between father and son was so deep. This was not going in the right direction.

I asked everyone to take a breath. Then I asked Robert if he loved Arthur. He said he did. So, I asked him to tell him so.

"I love you," Robert said.

"You don't," Arthur said. "I just don't understand. One minute he invites me in, the next he throws me out. I'm not your toy."

It was apparent to me that the more you love someone, the deeper the hurt is when you are estranged.

"I have not made a mistake intentionally," Robert said. "But I'm a regular human being and I . . ."

"But he's been homeless for three years," I said. "And you've been absent from his life. That's why he's so hurt."

"I understand," Robert said. And then he turned to his son. "Arthur, listen, I love you. I did all my life. I apologize. I'm sorry. Please forgive me, can you?"

Arthur teared up.

I asked Arthur not to promise anything, just to keep an open mind.

"For you, I will." Then father and son embraced. That was the first glimmer of hope.

Things may have only moved an inch, but they moved.

After that, my family pitched in to help in other ways. Marissa, my daughter, spoke to our friends Donna and Bill Benell, who had a beautiful spare apartment in a house they owned. They made it available to Arthur. My son David contacted Michael Sabitoni, who led the Laborers International Union in Rhode Island, and set up a meeting with Arthur.

After the meeting, they found him a union job in maintenance that paid $25 an hour, plus generous benefits, including health care, overtime, and a pension plan.

Arthur was humbled by the people who came forward to help him.

"I never realized there's so many people . . . [who want to help me]," Arthur said. "I haven't been so happy in my life. But I consider all these people now family—100 percent."

Arthur was a good person who had been sucker punched by life. He didn't see a way out of his situation. He had an awful attitude about his life, and he had cut off connections from everyone, including his father, whom he blamed for not helping him. And he was not helping himself, almost to spite his father.

Once Arthur was willing to ask for help, once he was willing to forgive his father, Arthur found a way back to a productive life.

Arthur never missed a day of work and very quickly he was paying rent to the Benells. And occasionally, he would stop by our house for Sunday dinner.

With the "Armenian Assassin" Arthur Saribekian

What we were able to show Arthur, a lesson I hope that everyone can learn, is that if you ask for help, it is almost always available. And doing a little, even just showing that you care, can make a huge difference in someone's life.

Arthur's situation required a great deal of compassion on the part of our family and that of others like the Bennels, but it required understanding from Arthur's father and Arthur himself to repair the breach and forge a new path.

Be Somebody

I want to leave you with a final case that touched me most deeply. It involved Jose Jimenez, a man who came before me a few years ago. He had two parking tickets, one recent and one from five years before.

He was not aware of the one from five years earlier. As for the recent one, Jose explained that he had a landscaping business and that he was driving his truck from work. He came home late one night, and his tenant was having a party so there was no parking available at the building. Rather than cause a stir, he parked on his street, which was not a legal spot for overnight parking. He figured he would move his car later. He went inside, had dinner, and was so tired that he fell asleep on the couch. When he woke up and went outside to move his truck, he had a ticket.

Jose said he had paid the $20 ticket fee, but the city said they had received the payment late and was now charging him more. He was hoping that I would accept that he had already paid the ticket.

I told him that his file showed the ticket had been paid. There was a penalty, but I was willing to waive that. I told him, "You're free to go."

But he wasn't finished. There was something he needed to tell me. "I want to tell you something about my life," he said.

"I want to say thank you," Jose told me. "Twenty years ago, I was a bad boy."

It turned out that this was not the first time he had appeared before me. Twenty years before, he had been on a bad path in life. He would turn up in court every month with a speeding ticket or other violations.

I certainly didn't recognize him. Jose was eighteen years old the first time he came before me.

I can't even say I recall the advice I gave him at the time because it is the same advice I give to many young people in his situation.

As he recalled it, what I said to him then was what I say to many young men and women who were headed down the wrong path. I asked them, simply, "How do you want to turn out?"

Sometimes I continued, as I did with this man when he was eighteen. I said, "From where I'm sitting, you have three choices for your future. You could end up dead, in prison, or you can be somebody. The choice is yours."

"I told you: I want to be somebody," Jose said, tearing up. Then he explained that he got his commercial driving license, became a truck driver, and became an American citizen sixteen years ago. He choked back tears as he pulled his passport from his back pocket and showed it to me.

This man then let me know that that simple sentence from me changed the course of his life. Twenty years earlier, he left my courtroom and decided to be somebody, and now here he was all this time later, married with children, a steady job, and a business. He owned a landscaping company and was doing well. He was working hard but living a good life.

There is an important lesson in this. Sometimes a person reaches a fork in the road where they have to make a choice. And sometimes all it takes to make the right choice is for someone to put a hand on their shoulder. That is all. It's transformational. You do not have to do handstands. You do not have to give millions of dollars. Sometimes, it is just telling a person that there's a different way, and that you can see them on that different path.

I asked him to come up to the bench, and we hugged.

And on that day, twenty years earlier, I put my hand on his shoulder.

Shaking hands with Jose Jimenez

Acknowledgments

Without Joyce, my wife, none of my accomplishments would be possible, and without my children, Frank, David, John, Marissa, and Paul, none of it would have any meaning. Without my brother Joe, *Caught in Providence* would never have happened.

I thank my grandparents for having the courage to leave Italy and settle in Providence, and I have to thank Providence, the city I love, and Federal Hill, my neighborhood, for the life my family has been able to enjoy here. My sincere thanks to the people of Providence, and all who made the Providence Municipal Court a beacon of hope and compassionate justice that has resonated around the world.

I thank Maggy Wilkinson of Athena Global Advisors for spearheading my writing of this book, my sons Frank and David for helping me through the many drafts, and Tom Teicholz for helping me tell my story and those of the incredible people who appeared in my courtroom. I want to thank my agents David Vigliano and Thomas Flannery Jr. of Vigliano Associates, and the team at BenBella, including editor-in-chief Leah Wilson, editor Vy Tran, and the publicity and marketing team. Any success this book has is also theirs; the mistakes or failures are all mine.

Compassion in the courtroom has made a difference in thousands of lives. In my experience, having compassion in your life is transformative.

About the Author

Judge Frank Caprio became an unexpected television and internet superstar while in his eighties! Judge Caprio's three-time Emmy-nominated television show, *Caught in Providence*, has amassed over 20 million followers across social media, and his videos have accrued billions of views. His compassionate temperament—unique for a judge—has earned him the title "the nicest judge in the world."

A beloved Rhode Island–based judge and attorney, Caprio is from humble beginnings. His parents were immigrants from Italy who, through hard work, devotion to family, and love of their new country and community, forged a new life in America. Their sense of responsibility and commitment to service and education was firmly instilled in each of their three sons. Today, Judge Caprio has inspired the world and become the face of compassionate justice.

Learn more at frankcaprio.com.